History Fair Workbook

A Manual for Teachers, Students, and Parents

Carlita Kosty

The Scarecrow Press, Inc.
Lanham, Maryland, and Oxford
2002

SCARECROW PRESS, INC.

Published in the United States of America
by Scarecrow Press, Inc.
A Member of the Rowman & Littlefield Publishing Group
4720 Boston Way, Lanham, Maryland 20706
www.scarecrowpress.com

PO Box 317
Oxford
OX2 9RU, UK

ISBN 0-8108-4487-7 (pbk. : alk. paper)

⊖™The paper used in this publication meets the minimum requirements of
American National Standard for Information Sciences—Permanence of
Paper for Printed Library Materials, ANSI/NISO Z39.48-1992.
Manufactured in the United States of America.

To Jean Flynn and Sylvia Swayne,
who helped me start my first History Fair
in 1987

Contents

VII. Advanced Competition

Appendixes

I. Introduction

About This Book

The *History Fair Workbook* was developed to teach a research skills unit while participating in the National History Day program. It offers the history teacher a complete curriculum unit as well as the resources to run a campus History Fair. The activities, forms, and handouts are simple and ready-to-use. For History Fair students and their parents, this book serves as a supplement to classroom instruction. It provides depth and detail not possible in many history courses.

Resources Include

- Information about History Fair, the National History Day competition, and how to use the program to teach research.

- Classroom management tools and schedules.

- Activities, worksheets, and rubrics to grade both process and product.

- Handouts explaining research skills and presentation techniques, both general and category specific.

- Ideas and guidelines for using the Internet in History Fair research.

- Forms and checklists for campus History Fair competition.

- Suggestions, advice, sample letters, and permission slips for advanced competition.

- Resource and topic lists, judging forms, bibliographies, and examples.

What Is History Fair?

History Fair is a national program that begins competition each school year at the campus level and ends with the National History Day contest. Students choose a topic which fits an annual theme, research for several weeks or months, then present their projects in one of four formats: a museum-style exhibit, a historical paper, an original live performance, or an electronic medium documentary. Participating in the History Fair program requires students to learn and practice important research skills and encourages the development of communication and organization competence. The History Fair used as a unit of study also meets state and national teaching standards.

The National History Day program began in 1974 when David Van Tassel, a history professor at Case Western Reserve University, organized a Cleveland-area history project competition in hopes of increasing interest in the study of history. Eventually Dr. Van Tassel obtained a grant from the National Endowment for the Humanities to make the program nationwide. The first national contest was held at Georgetown University in Washington, D.C., in 1980. Since 1992 National History Day has been based at the University of Maryland at College Park with Dr. Cathy Gorn serving as executive director since 1995.

Each year several million secondary school history students participate in the History Fair program, 500,000 of them in competition beyond the district level, and approximately 2,500 contestants convene each June for the four-day National History Day (NHD) competition in Maryland. NHD also hosts teacher institutes based on the upcoming year's theme and focused on using primary sources in the classroom as well as in project development. A number of NHD publications are available for teachers and students as well as an online educators' forum. NHD enjoys a close relationship with the National Archives and Records Administration which presents workshops for teacher-coaches during the national competition, and the National Archives website has a section specifically designed for use by History Fair participants. All activities and events are funded through grants, donations, entry fees, and advertising in NHD publications. While some senior division national winners receive college scholarships, the real prize for each student participant is the learning—the acquired skills, the increased competency, and the personal growth.

History Fair is both a structured program for teaching research, writing, and presentation skills, and a national competition. Teachers use the program for classroom instruction, but its requirements call for the students to get out into the community as well as do traditional research in the library or electronically on the Internet. Students benefit from challenging expectations and the opportunity to choose what interests them for a non-textbook experience with history.

History Fair is recognized throughout the United States as an exciting and challenging way to study history. Participation in History Fair fosters a history-consciousness in students that will serve them well all their lives. Teachers who elect to teach the program find the benefits well worth the extra time and energy required. This book is an attempt to make the teacher's task easier and more efficient, freeing time for work with individual students and their projects.

Why Teach History Fair?

The History Fair program is designed to capture student interest by allowing many choices in topic, format, and work groups while challenging student achievement with competition at a number of levels. It calls for the student's total involvement in content while the student is learning a multitude of skills simultaneously—learning as needed, not as part of instruction, often self-taught. These are real life skills: finding information; managing time and work partner relationships; accessing facilities beyond the school campus; evaluating the validity, relevance, and importance of information; organizing and creating a coherent and factual presentation; and making a story both instructive and entertaining.

History Fair is an equal opportunity competition. Boys and girls do equally well. There is no one ethnic or racial group that has an advantage. At advanced levels of competition students from wealthy school districts or prestigious private schools are frequently outdone by students from urban public schools or students who were home schooled. There are bright, talented, and competitive students from every school. This program brings out the best of those qualities. But average and struggling students often do very well, far better than their test scores might suggest, because they enjoy the process and are engaged in their chosen topic. Participation in a History Fair proves that all students can learn critical-thinking skills.

Most classroom teachers now must structure their lessons to meet district or state standards. More and more, student mastery of these standards is assessed on a mandated exam and teachers are held responsible for student performance. The History Fair program provides an excellent framework for teaching the knowledge and skills required to meet most social studies standards, in addition to many reading, writing, and technology standards. Students do authentic research in a variety of media, evaluate and synthesize information, write scripts, captions, or papers, and develop annotated bibliographies. This is alternative assessment at its best. Teachers whose classes participate in History Fair at some level find that their students do better on standardized tests, are more confident of their own abilities, and develop an abiding interest in history and current events. They may not remember much about a unit of instruction that the teacher spent many hours preparing, but they will always remember the History Fair project they did.

The History Fair program easily adapts to team teaching or interdisciplinary instruction. Indeed, the most logical and beneficial plan is cross-curricular cooperation among a student's teachers, allowing the student an opportunity for credit in multiple classes while mastering essential skills from several disciplines. Outside the classroom this program encourages family and community engagement as students explore local history topics or consult experts, visit museums, investigate archives, or conduct oral history interviews.

This workbook is designed to guide the History Fair teacher through the sometimes daunting task of managing a major research project with several classes of students and a variety of topics. It provides a wide choice of approaches and levels of involvement. Parents will find the suggestions, handouts, and worksheets helpful in guiding their children through the process. In addition, both parent and teacher will gain a comprehensive understanding of what the program involves and how to best use it to help their students develop important skills for the future.

How to Use This Workbook

Most of the activities, forms, suggestions, and handouts included in this workbook were developed through use in middle school classrooms. Others were created for teacher workshops on using the History Fair program. Many were originally designed to be overhead projector transparencies. The purpose is to provide classroom teachers with a ready-to-use research project curriculum/manual based on the National History Day program.

Whether or not the students actually participate in the National History Day competition, the program itself is an excellent framework for history research projects. It provides rules, strategies, and objectives, and gives students a variety of presentation formats to meet their talents and interests. Indeed, first-time teachers may want to have only a campus fair the first year. That said, it must be pointed out that taking students to regional and state competitions is probably the best way to inspire them to do better. They can hear it from teachers over and over, but seeing other students' work is what seems to matter.

The parent of a student participant, whether through a history class at school or from a home school, will find the activities and handouts easy to understand and use. Although the Project Progress Reports were designed to give middle school teachers a way to grade the process of research and preparation, the reports can just as easily be used as guides through the various stages of the project. Likewise, the handouts on various aspects of research and project production give the student access to ideas and techniques that improve both the student's skills and understanding and the quality of the project.

The items are organized into the following sections:

In the Classroom contains forms and suggestions for classroom and project management.

Grading the Process provides a selection of activities called Project Progress Reports (PPRs) which help the teacher grade students daily or weekly as they progress through the stages of their research project. There are also model tests and rubrics to grade the final project.

Student Research and Presentation offers a selection of handouts for student use in research or project development. Some deal with very specific parts of the process. Teachers may want to keep several copies on hand to be given out as students need them.

Using the Internet is a mini-unit for student research on the World Wide Web. It contains several useful handouts, review for the pros, and the basics for beginners. The Consider the Source worksheet is an excellent critical-thinking activity.

Campus Fair Administration includes forms and suggestions to plan, organize, and run a campus History Fair.

Advanced Competition contains suggestions and handouts for students and parents. Also, several sample letters and permission forms teachers may find useful.

In the **appendix** teachers will find a chart comparing national teaching standards with NHD objectives; a bibliography of suggested primary source collections for the school library; a list of resources for classroom instruction or campus History Fair administration; two sample process narratives by NHD finalists; topic lists from previous years; official NHD judging forms; and a glossary of History Fair terms.

No one teacher could possibly use all the forms in this book. The variety allows teachers great flexibility in lesson planning and level of class involvement. The activities, or PPRs, are designed to both check on student progress and help the student with the project.

History Fair
General Information

History Fair is an exciting way to study history, learn about issues, events, ideas, and people while also learning valuable lifetime skills. History Fair lets you choose an interesting topic related to an annual theme in the category—exhibit, paper, performance or documentary—that fits both your topic and your personal style. Your success in producing a History Fair entry may even take you to National History Day.

Annual Schedule

September/October	Explore topics, search for sources
December to February	RESEARCH, RESEARCH, RESEARCH Complete projects and paperwork Hold school fairs and district fairs
February to April	Regional History Day Competition
April/May	State History Day Competition
Second week of June	National History Day, University of Maryland at College Park

*At each level of competition the first and second prize winners
in each category, plus certain special award recipients,
are eligible to advance to the next level.*

Annual Themes

2003	Rights and Responsibilities in History
2004	Exploration, Encounter, Exchange in History
2005	Communication in History: The Key to Understanding
2006	Taking a Stand in History: People, Places, Ideas
2007	Triumph and Tragedy in History
2008	The Individual in History

National History Day Address

National History Day
0119 Cecil Hall
University of Maryland
College Park, MD 20742
(301) 314-9739
www.nationalhistoryday.org
national.history.day@umail.umd.edu

Ask for:
1. annual *Curriculum Book*
2. *National History Day Rule Book*

History Project Skills Profile

Finding Information and Deciding What to Do with It

- Research, including library, museum, primary sources
- Primary source location, interpretation, and use
- Telephone inquiry
- Internet inquiry
- Interview, oral history
- Evaluating sources: validity, importance, fact v. opinion, bias
- Making generalizations and forming opinions
- Note taking and summarization
- Finding main ideas, drawing conclusions, supporting with details
- Organization, outlining
- Supporting generalizations and opinions with historical fact
- Bibliography (and acknowledgments or credits)

Presentation Skills

- Organization and layout
- Focus and theme
- Nonfiction writing (narrative, captions, scripts, annotations)
- Editing, revising
- Demonstration of mastery
- Use of illustrations, graphics, color, and other visuals to complement and enhance presentations
- Developing finished products in various formats: written, dramatic, electronic, visual

Interpersonal and Social Skills

- Time management, schedules and deadlines
- Group work/shared responsibility
- Choosing appropriate partners or groups
- Consensus and making group decisions
- Telephone manners and voice, interviewing
- Dealing with adults other than school personnel

For a detailed comparison of National History Day objectives and the National Council for the Social Studies Standards see Correlation of Objectives and Standards in the appendix.

II. In the Classroom

How to Use the Items in This Section

For the Classroom Teacher

Careful class management is critical. Teaching a unit of study with every student on a different topic can be intimidating and exhausting even for the experienced teacher. The handouts and forms in this section simplify and organize the process. Keeping students organized, on task, and on schedule is the primary goal addressed.

A typical History Fair research project would include the following stages:
1. Topic exploration and preliminary skills lessons. Students choose topics and decide whether to work in a group or alone. (1 to 2 weeks)
2. Research in a variety of media—background, secondary sources, then primary sources. (3 to 6 weeks)
3. Evaluation of material, organization and planning or outlining. (1 week)
4. Project production. (1 to 3 weeks)
5. Paperwork: Process narrative and annotated bibliography. (1 week)
6. Present projects during class or at campus competition.

For the Parent or Student

Although this section of the *History Fair Workbook* is intended specifically for classroom teachers, there are several handouts that may be of particular interest to parents or students. **Develop a Topic List** explains the concept of choosing a topic that fits the annual NHD theme and offers many places to look for good topics. **Choices** helps the student to decide on the appropriate category for the topic and the student's own talents. The **History Fair General Information** handout gives an annual schedule plus a summary of the National History Day rules. (In addition, all students should have access to the *National History Day Rule Book* in the classroom or have a copy of their own. See Resources in the appendix for more information.)

In This Section

Finding Time in the Curriculum is an outline of models teachers may follow when planning a research unit or participating in the History Fair program.

Organize the Classroom is a checklist for teachers.

Some Hints to Consider lists a few details and extras that teachers can do to make the History Fair unit go smoothly and help students produce excellent projects.

Develop a Class Topic List explains the History Fair annual theme and why topic choice is so important in project development. It includes ways teachers can create and adapt topic lists to their own students, locale, and curriculum.

Choices—Topic, Category, Group? The decisions students make early in the research process are vitally important. This handout gives students, parents, and teachers some questions to consider and it is easily adaptable to an overhead transparency.

History Research Project T-chart provides the teacher with a way to differentiate assignments allowing some students to compete in the History Fair and others the option of not competing. This T-chart is one model of assignment differentiation.

Sample Letter to Parents with Permission Return Form is an example for the teacher to use as a guide in communicating with parents. Making sure the parents are informed and gaining their support is especially important with middle school classes.

The **Group Project Contract** is designed to make students take group choices seriously and prevent personality conflicts during the project. It should be used with the **History Fair Log Sheet**.

The **History Fair Timeline and Rules Summary** is a general handout for all participants at the beginning of the project. Fill in the information and dates for your campus or district and the current year's History Fair theme.

The **History Research Paper: Instructions and Deadlines** is an assignment model for the non-competition project if the teacher offers this option to some students.

Teacher's Project Checklist is a class assignment management tool. Teachers may also use this form on an overhead transparency.

Finding Time in the Curriculum
Strategies to Include History Fair in Social Studies Classes

I. Considerations

    A. How to Correlate with Standards or Curriculum?
    The History Fair program teaches many, if not most, of the research, critical-thinking, and nonfiction writing skills required today by state and district standards and curriculum.

    B. Finding Time to Include with Required Course Content
        1. Teach a content unit and work on History Fair projects simultaneously, dividing class time between the two on a regular schedule.
        2. Compact content curriculum to create a four to six week block for teaching a research unit using the History Fair program as the model.

II. Strategy Options

    A. Teach a Research Unit
        1. All students do a project, but History Fair competition is by choice.
        2. Skills lessons and research/production time in class.
        3. Topics of choice, no restrictions other than theme (or limit to curriculum content).
        4. Maximum teacher control.

    B. Team Teach Interdisciplinary Unit
        1. Research and organization in language arts or reading class.
        2. Bibliography and process paper in English class or language arts.
        3. Project production and presentation in history or social studies class.
        4. Multi-class involvement increases student focus and aids skills development.

    C. Teach Curriculum Unit via Research Projects
        1. Students choose topics from unit list (e.g., Industrial Revolution).
        2. Share results/information in class.
        3. Teach research skills without sacrificing time on course content.
        4. Limited topic choice may influence student interest.

    D. With Only Honors or Gifted & Talented Students, Limited Class Time
        1. Assumes a high level of student skill and dedication.
        2. Leaves out qualified and interested students in regular classes.
        3. Limited student guidance, limited control by teacher.
        4. Opportunity for more parent involvement.

Organize the Classroom
A Teacher Checklist

1. Get the support of the principal—Talk about curriculum standards, skills that raise test scores, and alternative assessment.

2. Check with other teachers before scheduling due dates—Avoid assigning students two or more major projects due the same week.

3. Plan with the librarian—Schedule days in the library and find out about sources available and the policy on copies for students. Discuss bibliography style choice.

4. Reserve the Computer Lab—Schedule days for students to search on the Internet and, later, word processing.

5. Do preliminary "prep" activities with students—Locating information, taking notes, summarization, supporting details, organization, etc. (reading skills, social studies skills)

6. Decide on requirements, length of unit, and deadlines—Create a timeline and share with the students and parents.

7. Let the parents know—Send home a letter or put an article in the parent newsletter, or both.

8. Organize the kids—Select topics and groups, distribute handouts. Make a calendar or timeline of due dates and deadlines.

9. Help students find primary sources—Use your library, community, and Internet resources.

10. Have examples available—Put together a notebook with sample Process Narratives and Annotated Bibliographies, also Historical Papers. Make a bulletin board and show slides/tapes/CDs of winning projects whenever possible.

11. Grade the process—Use Project Progress Report activities (PPRs) and participation grades for daily or weekly evaluation.

12. Allow class time to work—And encourage weekend meetings of groups and/or trips to libraries or museums.

13. Grade the final projects—Use a rubric or checklist *before* they are judged at competition, if possible. (Can be done after, if necessary.)

14. Share in class—Have students present their projects and/or do a debriefing of the process.

Some Hints to Consider
for Running an Effective History Fair Program

- Give out topic lists and hold a general question and answer session a week or two before formally beginning the project or taking the class to the library to explore possible topics.

- Set rules and schedules early. Post them in the classroom. Also post copies of assignment worksheets (PPRs) with due dates so students can check without asking the teacher.

- Prepare an introductory packet for students to take home. Good items to include are the General Information, Timeline and Rules Summary handout sheet, the Choices handout, a letter to parents, Getting the Details handout on note-taking, the Primary and Secondary Sources T-chart, and Helpful Hints for Winning Projects. Also include a current topic list if not provided earlier.

- Try rearranging desks in the classroom to make group consultation and/or use of resources more convenient.

- Compile a notebook with examples of Process Narratives and Annotated Bibliographies for students to look at. Be sure to note what the annual theme was at the time the example was written.

- Make a bulletin board or keep a scrapbook with snap shots of previous school or district fairs and winners. Also instructive are photos of winning exhibits and a copy of the official rules.

- Have a local telephone directory in class as well as those for nearby large cities and the state capital.

- It's OK to interfere when students want to interview important or famous people. Teachers can pave the way with a brief phone call or e-mail. Most people are more than willing to help students in any way they can.

- Be lenient in grading, at least at first. The skills required for quality History Fair projects are difficult concepts and few students have experience with "real" research. The goal is to encourage, not discourage.

- Although students often focus on the competition, teachers should stress the learning, the new experiences, and the exposure to real-life problem solving.

- Expect to spend time working with individual students or project groups. Possibly arrange regular before or after school sessions for History Fair consultations.

- Enlist the assistance of other faculty to advise students: the drama coach for performances; the computer teacher or A/V technician for documentaries; an art teacher for exhibits; and an English or journalism teacher for papers.

- Compile a database of local area historical societies, civic groups museums, special libraries, ethnic or cultural organizations, and so on, that may be helpful.

Develop a Class Topic List

The National History Day annual theme is usually so general that any topic will fit if the story is developed from the proper perspective. Students who insist on popular topics such as the Civil War, the Civil Rights Movement, or Nazi Germany, can almost always find a way to "make it fit." However, the true competitor will look for a unique topic or an unusual approach to a traditional one. The teacher should create a topic list that meets student interest and curriculum restraints, and includes local topics.

National History Day publishes a short essay each year explaining the theme and suggesting topics. It is available on their website, in the NHD *Annual Curriculum Book*, and copies are frequently handed out at the previous season's State History Day competition. Students and teachers will notice that the theme can be approached very broadly, even creatively. Some teachers find that with younger students it is helpful for teachers to prepare and distribute a simplified, less abstract version of this handout.

Because NHD themes are often recycled, sample topic lists for a number of themes are included in the appendix. Use the following suggestions to develop a customized list. Remember, the student's choice of a topic is probably the most important step in the History Fair project. Although History Fair topic lists are usually intended to inspire further exploration by the student, the reality is that most students choose topics from the list their teacher gives them.

Brainstorm with the class: After discussing the meaning(s) of the theme, and possibly defining its vocabulary using a dictionary, write headings for different disciplines on the board. Those might include Politics, Science, Art & Music, Religion, Technology & Invention, Commerce. Then have the class suggest topics while teacher lists them under the appropriate heading. As with most brainstorming activities, this is not the time to edit out unsuitable or impossible ideas.

Start with the obvious: Every theme will suggest a few really well known and popular topics. Start with these, even though they may seen too elementary. Obvious topics will demonstrate to the student what does and does not fit the theme and will serve as a starting point for investigation. Less creative or beginning students may do very well with one of these topics.

Use the National History Day Annual Curriculum Book and/or National History Day website: Each year the National History Day office publishes a magazine featuring the current theme. It contains lists of suggested topics, bibliographies (including websites), and articles by professional historians on research techniques and selected topics. In addition, the NHD website offers a good general topic list. Make use of these valuable resources, adapting them as appropriate. The *Annual Curriculum Book* must be ordered from the national office or obtained at a teacher workshop.

Look for local history and special sources: Check the museums, libraries, and historical organizations in the area, they frequently have special collections or unusual sources that will suggest topics. Cultural heritage and living history associations are also useful for topic ideas. Choosing a little known person or event can work well if the student is able to show how the local topic was representative of something happening nationwide.

Pay attention to anniversary celebrations: It seems like every week or so there is another anniversary of a historical event or a famous person's birthday or death. Often these media events include articles in newspapers or magazines, opening of new museums or exhibits and even television documentaries. They provide excellent topic choices as the sources for research are readily accessible and the impact or legacy is widely discussed. A good example of this phenomenon was the 1998 NHD theme of Migrations which coincided with the sesquicentennial celebration of the Mormon trek to Utah in 1848.

Consider special curriculum restrictions: Because of time or curriculum restraints, teachers may need to limit the choice of topics to the content area of the class. Thus, American history students may be limited to topics in American history, government students may be restricted to topics in politics or government, and so forth. If this is the situation, consult the index of the textbook for suggested topics.

Consult the school librarian: Especially with younger students and in schools that serve lower socioeconomic populations, the school library will be the primary research facility. The librarian knows what materials are available and can help suggest appropriate topics and recommend elimination of those for which local resources are inadequate.

Collect ideas over several months: The best time to start on next year's topic list is just as soon as this year's contest is over, maybe even before. State competition events usually include workshops, discussion sessions, or teacher handouts which elaborate on the upcoming theme and suggest possible topics. Start a topic-list-in-progress, adding to it as things come to mind from news items, current events, or other sources. When it's time to actually start teaching in the fall, teachers will have a substantial topic list that has been developed specifically for the local area and students.

Be wary of current events and controversial topics: Except in rare instances, current or controversial topics seldom make good projects for a number of reasons. Long-term effects are difficult to see if the event is still in progress. Reliable, unbiased sources are hard to find. Frequently, the material available is incomplete or documents have not been released. In-depth analysis and a balanced presentation, two of the goals for History Fair projects, are extremely difficult to achieve. In addition, judges often have strong personal opinions on these topics. Of course, there are always exceptions. If teachers decide to allow students to pursue such a topic, it should be handled with great care and close supervision. The finished project must offer balance and historical perspective.

National History Day Annual Themes
(Dates refer to the spring semester contest season.)
2002—Revolution, Reaction and Reform in History
2003—Rights and Responsibilities in History
2004—Exploration, Encounter, Exchange in History
2005—Communication in History: The Key to Understanding
2006—Taking a Stand in History: People, Places, Ideas
2007—Triumph and Tragedy in History
2008—The Individual in History

Choices—Topic, Category, Group?

I. Selecting a Topic

1. Choose **something you LIKE**—you will be spending a lot of time with it. (Consider your own hobbies, interests, heroes, favorite movies, books.)

2. Your topic MUST relate to this year's **theme**:

   _____

3. Narrow your topic to something you can handle in approximately four to six weeks of research.

4. Do you have, or can you easily locate, **at least two good primary sources** for your topic?

5. **Suggestions**:
   - Choose the unusual rather than the obvious.
   - Look to your own family, friends, school, neighborhood, or church.
   - Local history is always good, and primary sources are usually available.
   - Ask your parents for ideas.
   - Check for Special Award categories that automatically send winning projects on to the next level of competition.
   - Use diagrams or graphic organizers to define and focus the topic you choose. Show concepts and connections.

6. **Ask**:
   - Can I show the historical context for this event?
   - Can I say something about this subject that few other people would know?
   - Can I explain what difference it made as well as what happened?
   - Can I tell the story from both sides?
   - Can I show cause and effect? Impact and significance? Change over time?
   - Can I relate my topic to other important historical events?
   - Can I show the impact of my topic on history?

**NO CHANGES AFTER _____

II. Choosing a Category: Exhibit? Paper? Performance? or Documentary?

1. What are **your own talents**? Do you write well? Are you artistic? Do you like to perform? Are you good with electronic or computer equipment?

2. What **kinds of sources** have you found?
   - Lots of good pictures suggests exhibit or documentary.
   - Excellent written primary sources suggests performance (incorporate the characters' actual words into dialogue) or paper.

3. **Play the Odds:** The most popular category, and most difficult to win, is Exhibits. The least popular are Individual Performance and Papers, but they require really good acting or writing skills. Documentary categories usually have few entries, but call for special skills and talents. Individual categories are less popular than group categories, but they tend to attract the truly serious competitors.

**NO CHANGES AFTER _____

III. Choosing a Group (optional)

1. Be careful about whom you work with: this is **your grade** you are dealing with. Remember: Requirements for your class project grade increase with additional group members. Also consider how a partner might be in advanced competition should you win.

2. Do you have **similar interests**?

3. Do you have **complementary skills and assets?**
   Writing? Art? Word processing/computer skills? Telephone? Parents willing to transport to libraries and/or interviews? Acting? Speaking voice?

4. Is each of your partners **reliable**? Do you know how to reach them by phone? Do they have regular school attendance? In advanced competition all group members must be present for judging.

5. Do your parents know each other? (This is especially helpful for transportation and weekend work sessions.)

6. Be very careful when choosing to work with friends. Make sure you can **work well together**. Many friendships have ended during a History Fair project. Partners should have similar work habits and goals.

**NO CHANGES AFTER _____

History Research Project T-chart

You MUST choose either the History Fair or a Research Paper.
Each student will work on one project /one topic for this unit.

History Fair

1. Extra credit (+5 pts. on avg) if project is completed and entered.

2. Topics must fit the theme:
   _____
   _____

3. Individuals or groups up to five students in Exhibits, Performances, or Documentaries. Papers are individuals only.

4. History Fair will require research and preparation OUTSIDE of class.

5. Category choices: Exhibit, Paper, Performance or Documentary.

6. Minimum of five sources: one must be primary; no encyclopedias. (Requirements increase for groups.)

7. Follow national rules for your chosen category.

8. Deadline: _____
   (Late projects will become research papers. No projects accepted after the campus History Fair.)

Research Paper

1. Basic requirement for all students NOT doing History Fair.

2. _____ topics only.

3. Individuals only.

4. Most work CAN be done in class if you use your time wisely and efficiently.

5. Papers only.

6. Minimum of three sources; only one may be an encyclopedia.

7. Minimum of three pages, plus bibliography, outline, and illustrations.

8. Due _____.
   Late projects accepted through
   _____ with penalty.

(date)

Dear Parent,

The _____ history teachers are pleased to announce the Annual History Fair to be held on _____ . The theme for this year's competition is:

_____

History Fair is a national program which begins at the school level in January or February and ends with National History Day at the University of Maryland near Washington D.C., in June. Students choose research topics and work either individually or in groups of two to five. The final project may take the form of an exhibit, a paper, a documentary (slide show, video, or computer program), or a live performance. Each category has specific rules. Student participants have been given a summary of the national rules (or a copy of the official Contest Guide), this year's schedule of events, and a list of possible topics.

Your child will be participating in this event through his or her history class. Whether participation is by class requirement, or by choice for extra credit, please understand that it will demand time outside the classroom if it is to be done successfully.

There are some things you can do to help:
1. Once your child has chosen a topic, and possibly a group to work with, discourage changes.
2. If your child has chosen to work with a group, get to know the other students' parents.
3. Help your child set a work schedule and encourage him or her to stay on task.
4. Help your student arrange transportation to local libraries, museums, or for interviews, as appropriate to the topic chosen.
5. Remember that in some classes the majority of the six weeks' grades will be based on research project work, with the completed project as the six weeks' test.

Top winners in each category at the campus History Fair are eligible to advance to the District or Regional level in _____ on _____. Please plan to visit the _____History Fair in the _____ on _____evening, _____ from _____ to _____, or plan to see the winning Exhibits on display in the _____ through_____.

If you have questions, need help, or want clarification of a rule, please call the school at _____ and leave a message for your child's history teacher or for _____, the fair director.

Please sign and return the permission form attached for your child to participate. We thank you for your support.

History Fair Director: History Teacher:

_____   _____

Permission to Enter History Fair

I understand that my son/daughter will be participating in the _____
History Fair on _____.

I have read the information and rules and I understand what is involved in this program. I have discussed the requirements with my child. He/She has my permission to participate in the History Fair program.

Student Participant: _____

Signed: _____   Date: _____

Please print name: _____

Daytime phone _____   Evening phone _____

Group Project Contract

When choosing a project for the History Fair many decisions must be made. One of the most important is whether to work with a partner/group or to work alone. For all group projects each participating member must agree to the contract below.

> **Contract**—to draw together, to make a bargain; usually an agreement between two or more people to do something. (*Macmillan Dictionary,* 1977)

Contracts should not be taken lightly or entered into without thought.

It must be understood that each member of a group will receive individual grades on the Project Progress Reports and other daily grades during the project. Upon completion and presentation of the project, the group will assess time and effort contributed by each member and submit a recommended grade distribution to the teacher. To make this process more objective, each group member is asked to keep a History Fair Log Sheet to be turned in with the grade recommendations.

* * * * * * * * * * * * * * * * * * * *

We, the Undersigned, have made the decision to work together as a group on the project described below. We understand that each of us is responsible for the completion of the project.

Topic   Title   Category

_____   _____   _____

I pledge to my History Fair group that I will . . .

- Contribute my fair share of research and planning.

- Fulfill all my assigned duties to the best of my ability and in good humor.

- Do my fair share of unplanned chores or errands as they become necessary.

- Work/meet with my group after school or on weekends as needed (exchange phone numbers now if you haven't already done so).

- Meet with my group after the project is complete, but before we receive our grade, to agree on the percent of contribution in time and effort by each member.

- Cheerfully accept the group project grade, or my agreed-upon percent thereof, as awarded by my teacher.

Discussed and Signed on this Date: _____   Teacher: _____

Students: Parents:

_____   _____

_____   _____

_____   _____

_____   _____

History Fair Log Sheet

For_____

Dates: _____ to _____

All students working in groups must keep accurate records of time spent working on the project outside of class. Use as many pages as needed.

Day/Date	Time Spent	Activity/Chore	Location	I Was With? Alone?
_____	_____	_____	_____	_____
_____	_____	_____	_____	_____
_____	_____	_____	_____	_____
_____	_____	_____	_____	_____
_____	_____	_____	_____	_____
_____	_____	_____	_____	_____
_____	_____	_____	_____	_____
_____	_____	_____	_____	_____
_____	_____	_____	_____	_____
_____	_____	_____	_____	_____
_____	_____	_____	_____	_____
_____	_____	_____	_____	_____
_____	_____	_____	_____	_____
_____	_____	_____	_____	_____

Add times and enter below:

Total time logged: _____ **by** _____ **Signature** _____
(date)

History Fair
Timeline and Rules Summary

This Year's Theme: _____

Dates and Deadlines

_____ Choose topics and groups, and begin research.

_____ Last day to change topics or groups. Group contracts should be on file.

_____ Registration in History or Social Studies classes.

_____ All PAPERS (for Historical Paper category) should be complete and turned in to the history teacher for distribution to reader-judges.

_____ Exhibit projects will be set up for judging. Judging of Exhibits, Performances, and Documentaries will take place immediately after school. Open House for parents and students _____

_____ Winning Exhibit projects on display in _____

_____ District competition at _____

_____ Regional History Fair at _____

_____ State History Day in _____

General Rules for all Projects

1. Entrants present projects in one of seven categories:
   - Historical Paper—individuals only
   - Individual Exhibit
   - Individual (live)Performance
   - Individual Documentary (Documentary category includes video, slide show, or computer program.)
   - Group Exhibit
   - Group (live) Performance
   - Group Documentary
   - All entries are divided into Junior (grades 6 to 8) and Senior (grades 9 to 12) Divisions.
2. Awards for the campus fair will be made both by grade level and by category. First and second place winners will be eligible to advance to District or Regional competition. Special Awards will be considered for projects dealing with the following subjects:
   - African American History
   - Women's History
   - Oral History
   - Hispanic History
   - Colonial/Revolutionary America
3. The judges will rank projects based on these values:
   - Historical Quality (60%) Is it correct? Is it complete? Was research used appropriately?
   - Presentation (20%) Does it make sense? Does it look/sound good?
   - Theme & Rules (20%) Does the project make clear how the topic fits the annual theme? Are all category rules followed?
4. Projects must show how the topic fits the theme. Students should analyze the topic, not just report it.
5. Groups are limited to five students. All groups should have a contract on file with their history teacher. All members must participate, and for Group Performances or Group Documentaries, all members must be present for judging.

6. All projects, except Papers, must have a one-to-two page description of how the topic fits the theme and how the project was developed. This Process Narrative can be no more than 500 words in length.
7. All projects must have an Annotated Bibliography of at least five sources. Primary sources should be used if they are available and listed first. Form should follow Turabian or MLA style manual.
8. No student may participate in more than one project.
9. Entrants may NOT mix formats. (A Paper is a paper; an Exhibit is an exhibit.) Exceptions: Both Exhibits and Performances may include brief recorded parts—video and/or audio.
10. Students from all grade levels (6 to 12) are invited to enter. Individual teachers may set guidelines as to eligibility, topics, deadlines, etc. All work on the project must be done during the current school year.
11. Projects are the work of the students entering the fair and no one else. Parents, of course, should assist with transportation, advice, and encouragement.
12. Performance and Documentary entrants will be interviewed by the judges at the campus fair. All categories may be interviewed at advanced levels of competition.

Rules for Individual Categories

EXHIBIT: No larger than 40" wide, 30" deep, and 72" (6 ft.) tall when displayed. Must have a title that is clear and visible. All items should have typed captions. Student-composed words limited to 500. Does not include documents or quotes used in the exhibit; does include student message in any media device. Required paperwork includes the Process Narrative and the Annotated Bibliography.

PAPER: May be a historical essay or a creative interpretation such as a fictional journal. 1500 to 2500 words in length (approximately 6 to 10 pages typed). Must include an Annotated Bibliography of all sources used. May incorporate illustrations or include a short appendix of illustrations. Footnotes or endnotes required for all quotes (see your English teacher). Five copies—three for the judges, one for your teacher, and one for you. Papers should be typed, double-spaced, plain title page, no cover.

PERFORMANCE: Ten-minute time limit (plus 5 min. set-up and 5 min. take-down). Scripts must be original (may incorporate quotes). All props, equipment, costumes, etc., must be supplied by the student entrant(s). Title of project and names of student entrant(s) should be announced at the beginning of the presentation. Some special equipment is allowed if it is student operated. No written material is allowed other than the required Process Narrative and Annotated Bibliography.

DOCUMENTARY: Ten-minute time limit, including titles and credits. All Documentary presentations should be student produced, edited, and may NOT be interactive. Credit should be given for photos, music, etc., used in the project. Title and name(s) of entrant(s) must be announced at the beginning of the presentation. No written material is allowed other than the required Process Narrative and Annotated Bibliography.

Your teacher has a copy of the official National History Day rules. These should be consulted for detailed or technical questions. For more information see:

_____

History Research Paper
Instructions and Deadlines

1. Topics in _____ only.

2. Individuals only.

3. Students may not change topics after _____.

4. The project should be completed and turned in by_____.
   Projects accepted with late penalty until _____.

5. The project should have **both** a **title page** (which includes the title of the paper, the student's name and class, and the date) and an **outside cover.**

6. The required **outline** must match the paper.

7. The paper should be _____ **to** _____ **pages** in length and include both an introduction and a conclusion.

8. The project should include a **Bibliography** of all sources used in research. A minimum of three sources is required, only one of which may be an encyclopedia. All sources should be cited in proper bibliographic form and in alphabetical order.

9. **Extra Credit** may be given for:
   - Illustrated or decorated cover.
   - Including illustrations to supplement the paper such as maps, original drawings, charts, copies of photos, etc.
   - Typing the paper, including the bibliography.
   - Using additional sources and listing them properly in the Bibliography.
   - Turning the completed project in before the due date.

10. **The Final Project should be assembled in this order:**

   > **Title Page**
   > **Outline***
   > **Paper*** **(final draft only)**
   > **Illustrations** **(optional)**
   > **Bibliography***

Place in a wrap-around cover, stapled, braded, tied, or otherwise securely fastened.

*Indicates a "process" grade or PPR *before* the final project is assembled.

Teacher's Project Checklist

For _____(class)

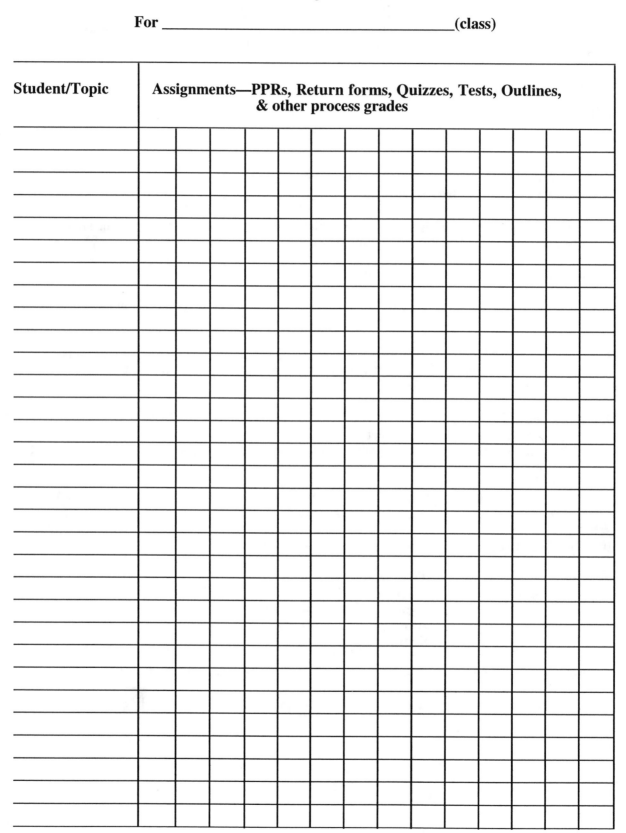

Student/Topic	Assignments—PPRs, Return forms, Quizzes, Tests, Outlines, & other process grades													

III. Grading the Process

How to Use the Items in This Section

For the Classroom Teacher

The classroom teacher's most common dilemma when embarking on a major project is how to give daily or weekly grades for the work students are doing and not have the entire grade depend on the final project. This set of Project Progress Report worksheets (PPRs) explains how to do the skills required, while providing the teacher with a format for grading student work regardless of topic, category, or stage of research. The PPRs also serve to keep the student on schedule. The final project evaluation sheets give the teacher a rubric to grade projects fairly, accurately, and objectively. Think of the PPRs as the daily grades and the completed project as the six weeks' test. If each component has been graded independently as part of the process, then students can correct problems before assembling the final product.

Bearing in mind that no teacher is expected to use all the PPRs, the following selections offer a variety of activities to choose from, depending on personal preference, time restraints, and curriculum requirements. Some items, such as the Primary Source Worksheet or the Independent Library Work PPR, can be used as often as desired or needed.

In addition to selected PPRs, teacher will probably want to check drafts of captions, papers or scripts, the Process Narrative, and the Annotated Bibliography. Ideally, every part of the project will have been graded individually before the students assemble the final presentation. This way, students have the opportunity to make all corrections before judging.

For the Parent or Student

Each PPR asks the student to practice a different research skill and many of them explain that skill in the content of the worksheet. The work students produce in the course of "doing" the assignment will help them later in the assembly of the project presentation, process narrative, or the annotated bibliography. For example, if a student completes the Annotated Bibliography PPR using a source from the student's research, then the student simply saves the worksheet until the bibliography is ready to type. In that same example, the student can also use the worksheet as a reference and example when researching and taking notes independently.

In This Section

Project Progress Report—Library Exploration is a simple way to grade a preliminary library day spent searching for topics, while requiring students to practice their bibliographic citation skills.

PPR—Topic Choice not only asks the student to commit to a topic, but the student must show basic understanding of what is involved in the story by listing subtopics, related topics, and key words or phrases to use in finding information. It also asks for an initial explanation of the History Fair theme as it relates to the topic chosen.

PPR—Proposal for Project Approval requires the student to plan the process of research and think through the idea of the topic focus and theme, as well as list two sources. This is a more in depth lesson than the Topic Choice PPR above and could be used instead, but only after students have had a week or so to get a handle on their topics.

PPR—My Research Plan is an effective way to get students to think about research outside the school library. The teacher could provide lists of local museums, libraries, universities, historic sites, etc., to help students brainstorm sources. One way to use this PPR is to send it home over a weekend and have parents offer suggestions. Asking parents to participate in this assignment also helps them understand the wide range of learning opportunities offered in the History Fair program.

PPR—Independent Library Work and **PPR—Independent Computer Lab Work** are simple forms for students to complete on their own, even at home. The activities can be used as often as needed and work well as extra credit offerings or make-up assignments. Hint: set a minimum time for credit, such as 30 or 45 minutes.

A Quiz! should be used after students have spent a few days in the library and had plenty of practice with bibliographic citation. Teacher should choose a book from the library and make a copy or transparency of the title page to use as the example for the quiz. The other questions deal with the vocabulary of library research.

PPR—The Annotated Bibliography explains the content requirements for annotations and asks the student to practice. This activity can be used along with handouts Make a Bibliography and The Annotated Bibliography which give examples for students to follow. (Found in the Student Research and Presentation section.)

The Primary Source Worksheet is a generic tool for analyzing any primary source, written or other format. By asking students questions *about* the source (date, purpose, creator, etc.) before attempting to extract information *from* the source, students can better understand what the source means to their topic. This activity also asks students to recognize bias, a frequent characteristic of primary sources. The Primary Source Worksheet may be used as often as needed. Indeed, some teachers insist that the student completes a worksheet for each primary source used. Later, the information is easily converted into annotations for the bibliography. (Note: Both NHD and the National Archives have developed a number of specialized forms in this style. Analysis worksheets specifically for photographs, maps, statistics, and other special sources can be found in NHD annual *Curriculum Book* and on the NARA website. See Resources in the appendix.)

PPR—Creating the Thesis Statement takes the student step by step through the process. Teachers need to supervise this activity closely as it is a difficult concept for many students and may require more time than one would expect. However, the effort in getting the student to understand focus and plan are well worth the time spent and will make the rest of the project go more smoothly.

PPR—Topic Timeline is the first activity that requires the student to organize information found in research. In this assignment students also place their topics in context of national or world events. If there are major gaps in the student's research, they should become obvious when making a timeline.

PPR—Plan an Exhibit gives instructions to prepare a "blueprint" of the exhibit. The more planning students do, the more professional the finished exhibit looks. Remind students that a bigger board is not always better; it depends on what is displayed *on* the board.

PPR—Make an Outline for the Historical Paper is a basic review of standard outline form. Students may need to practice this skill on something already written, like a section in their textbooks, before attempting to outline their own research information. Some teachers use "skeleton" outlines first, then ease students into outlining existing text.

PPR—Plan a Performance explains the process of creating a History Fair performance script. Students must include background information, tell the story, and use primary source quotes where appropriate.

PPR—Make a Documentary Storyboard shows students how to outline their presentation in terms or what they tell and what they show. Doing this activity gives them a basis for the script and a format for their pictures or video. They will probably discover that they need more visuals.

The **Research Skills Test** is an example of how teachers can test a class on this unit of study even though every student was working on a different topic. This particular sample was created for an eighth grade American history class and the objective part (pages one and two) is formatted to use Scantron answer sheets for quicker grading. Some teachers may opt to use the test as is, others will want to rewrite the first two pages using topics and examples from their own curriculum. The third page, which asks students to write about their own research, may be used by itself as a general check on progress. To give a reliable indication of student progress, the Research Skills Test should be given without allowing students to use their notes.

Evaluation rubric grade sheets for **Exhibits**, **Papers**, **Performances**, and **Documentaries**, give the teacher an objective format for grading the final project. It is suggested that the teacher also check rough drafts of both the Project Narrative and the Annotated Bibliography prior to project completion so that all parts of the project have been graded at least once before the finished product is assembled and submitted.

Research Paper Evaluation is the rubric to use for students who choose not to enter History Fair competition and have done a standard research paper instead. Teachers will want to modify criteria as needed to match the assignment as given.

PPR—Debrief the Project helps the students reflect on the entire project—what was done or left undone, what was learned, what was valuable, what should have been changed. These responses also help teacher plan for next year.

Project Progress Report
Library Exploration

1. A. The first topic I read about: _____

   B. The source I used was (author's name and other information about the book in proper bibliographic form, please)

     _____
     _____
     _____

   C. One fact I learned: _____
     _____
     _____

2. A. The second topic I read about: _____

   B. The source I used was

     _____
     _____
     _____

   C. One fact I learned: _____
     _____
     _____

3. A. The third topic I read about: _____

   B. The source I used was

     _____
     _____
     _____

   C. One fact I learned: _____
     _____
     _____

Project Progress Report
Topic Choice

1. My first choice topic is _____

2. I decided on this topic because (a sentence, please)

_____

_____

3. One subtopic **or** related topic is:

_____

4. Tell **how** the above is associated with your topic:
   (Using your answer from Ques. #3 above.)

_____

_____

5. Some key words, phrases, or names to look up are: _____

_____

_____

(for History Fair participants only)

6. My chosen topic fits the theme "_____"

   like this (explain in a paragraph): _____

_____

_____

_____

_____

Topic_____ Name_____ Date_____ Class_____

Project Progress Report
Proposal for Project Approval

1. State your complete topic: _____

2. What will be the focus of your project? This is the thesis sentence or main idea. Write **one sentence** below:

   _____

   _____

   _____

3. State two reasons why your topic (person, event, issue, etc.) is important in history. One sentence each, please. Consider long-term as well as immediate effects.

   a. _____

   b. _____

4. This year's History Fair theme is "_____"
   How does your topic fit this theme?

   _____

   _____

   _____

   _____

5. List (in proper bibliographic form, please) one good primary source you have found and one basic secondary work you will use.

   a. primary source: _____

   _____

   b. secondary source: _____

   _____

Topic_____ Name_____ Date_____ Class_____

My Research Plan

Well-balanced research includes a variety of sources; both primary and secondary; all sides of an issue; and collected from a number of locations. Please use the outline below to plan your own research on this project.

1. In the **school library** I will look for: _____

   _____

2. **Other libraries** I will visit: _____

   _____

3. **Museums or historical sites** I will visit: _____

   _____

4. Local **experts** I will interview: _____

   _____

5. People I intend to contact for **oral history** interviews: _____

   _____

6. **Websites** I intend to use: _____

   _____

7. **Magazines**, **journals**, or **newspapers** I intend to search: _____

   _____

   _____

8. **Other sources** I will use: _____

   _____

Topic_____ Name_____ Date_____ Class_____

Project Progress Report
Independent Library Work

1. How long were you in the library today? _____

2. What did you do today? (Check as many that apply.)

_____a. did research and took notes

_____b. located and checked out book(s)

_____c. looked for illustrations

_____d. checked information for bibliography

_____e. read reference book for background information on _____

_____f. checked library collection for primary sources

_____g. other_____

_____

3. State one thing you learned today:

_____

_____

_____

4. List one source you used today (in proper bibliographic form, please).

_____

_____

_____

Topic_____ Name_____ Date_____ Class_____

Project Progress Report
Independent Computer Lab Work

1. How long were you in the computer lab today? (in hours and/or minutes) _____

2. What did you do today? (Check as many as apply.)

_____a. research and notes

_____b. looked for illustrations

_____c. looked for primary sources

_____d. checked information for bibliography

_____e. word processing for—circle one or more:

title(s)   captions   project narrative   bibliography   script   paper

_____f. other (explain) _____

3. State one thing you learned today: (In a sentence, please.)

_____

_____

_____

4. What **program** or **source** did you use? (Sources in proper bibliographic form, please.)

_____

_____

_____

A QUIZ!!
(Bibliographic Citation)

Some teachers check notes as students work in the library to see if students are getting the correct bibliographic information in their citations. If there is not time to check each one's notes, after several days of library work, return to the classroom and give a quiz.

Choose a book from the library with a typical title page and make a transparency from it, enlarging if possible, to make it clearly legible on the overhead projector. Biographies work especially well if the subject is someone well-known to the students. Try to find one with the copyright date printed on the title page or write it on the transparency yourself. Then have the students pretend they are using this book for their research and write the appropriate citation following standard form.*

Also check vocabulary understanding at this point with the following matching exercise:

Library Research Vocabulary

____1. the subject you are researching

____2. a list of sources you use in research

____3. one place you find information on your subject

____4. the true story of someone's life

____5. the date a book was published

____6. an alphabetical listing of subjects in a book

____7. first-hand information from a witness or participant

____8. writing which is not historical fact

____9. a reference book containing general information about many topics

____10. a magazine, newspaper, or journal

A. biography

B. fiction

C. periodical

D. bibliography

E. encyclopedia

F. topic

G. source

H. copyright date

I. index

J. primary source

---

*Standard form: NHD rules state that students may use either Kate Turabian or MLA style and that consistency is the key. Since most historians seem to prefer Turabian, and many History Fair judges are history professors, Turabian is used in these lessons. (See handout in Section V, Student Research and Presentation.)

Project Progress Report
The Annotated Bibliography

1. Choose three sources you have used for research on this project. Try to make them different types of sources and include one primary source if possible. Cite the bibliographic information in standard form on the lines provided below.

2. Write a short, one to three sentence description of the source by answering the applicable questions below:
   - What kind of a source is it? (textbook? biography? interview? website? photograph? video documentary?)
   - What information or understanding did you gain from it?
   - If it is a primary source, what makes it primary to your topic?
   - If it is an interview, how is the person knowledgeable on your topic?
   - Did you discover a new aspect of your story or uncover interesting details?
   - Did this source lead you to other useful sources?
   - Did you locate this source under unusual circumstances?

1. (Citation) _____
   _____

   (Annotation) _____
   _____
   _____
   _____

2. (Citation) _____
   _____

   (Annotation) _____
   _____
   _____
   _____

3. (Citation) _____
   _____

   (Annotation) _____
   _____
   _____
   _____

Project Progress Report
Primary Source Worksheet

I. Item to be analyzed—give title or description: _____
Examine the item and answer the following questions:

1. Is there any introduction or explanation accompanying this item? If so, what does it tell you?
_____

2. What kind of item is this? (Circle one below.)

Map	Organization Publication	Newspaper	Business Records	Recording—video/audio
Lette	Government Document	Song/Poem	Advertisement	Collection/Scrapbook
Memoirs	Certificate or License	Poster	Illustration/Photo	Files
Book	Diary/Journal/Log	Artifact	Magazine Article	Other: _____

3. What is the date of the item? _____ If no date, what is your estimate? _____
What information do you base this on? _____

4. Who created the item? Or where did it come from? _____

5. For what audience or use is the item intended? _____

6. If written or recorded, is the item in its original language? _____ If no, explain below:
_____

7. Are there any unusual marks, seals, or notations? _____

II. What does this item tell you? Analyze the information you get from the item by answering the following questions:

1. How does this item relate to your topic? _____
_____

2. What does this item tell you about your topic? (Continue on back if more space is needed.)
a. _____
_____

b. _____
_____

c. _____
_____

3. Is there any evidence of bias or prejudice? _____ If so, give an example and/or explain:
_____
_____
_____

4. This source *contradicts   confirms   explains   expands*   (circle one) what I already know about my topic in the following way:
_____

Topic_____ Name_____ Date_____ Class____

Project Progress Report
Creating the Thesis Statement

After you have chosen a topic and done preliminary research in several secondary sources such as encyclopedias or textbooks, you are ready to write a thesis statement. Follow the steps below.

1. Think of a question that you want to answer in your research.
   - This should be a "why" or "how" question—why or how something happened, not what happened.
   - It should be a broad question, not a detail.
   - It should be a question that has several possible answers.

   _____

   _____

   _____

2. Based on what you already know about your topic, how would you answer the question above? This an hypothesis, or educated guess, about what the answer to your question will be.
   - This answer should be arguable as it probably includes your opinion.
   - It should focus on the part of your story you want to emphasize in your project.
   - It should show the importance of the event or issue in history.

   _____

   _____

   _____

3. Now, combine the question and answer into one sentence. This is your Thesis Statement. It will be the focus of your research and the point of your project.

   _____

   _____

   _____

   _____

   _____

Hints
   - Use some of the vocabulary from this year's theme in your thesis statement.

   - Find out what others have said about this event or issue and focus your research either to prove or disprove their arguments.

   - Be open to new ideas as you research. Don't be afraid to prove your hypothesis wrong. You can always revise and refine the thesis statement to reflect your findings later.

Project Progress Report
Topic Timeline

Make a Timeline of Your Topic:

1. Choose at least five events in your topic and arrange them in order. If your topic **is** an event, then choose parts of the event or events leading up to and/or resulting from your main topic event.

2. Choose at least two events that are external to your topic - that is, not part of your topic. Try to make them well-known national or world events that most people would recognize.

3. Make a vertical timeline with the five "topic events" on the left side and the two "external events" on the right. (You may have up to ten on the left and five on the right if you wish.) The point of this exercise is to focus on the sequence of events in your topic and to give it context within national or world history.

4. Label the top of your timeline with the beginning date (five to ten years before your topic) and the ending date (five years or more after your topic). Then space out the years in **regular** intervals (like inches on a ruler).

5. Enter your information at the correct dates and in short-form (do not have to be in complete sentences—make the entries more like headlines). Make sure that the events you enter are things you will cover in your project presentation.

6. Always give your timeline a title (probably the same as your topic).

7. See the example below on the **Declaration of Independence.**

(topic events)	**1760**	(world events)
	17 63	British win the French & Indian War.
Stamp Act Congress is first organized protest.	17 65	
First Continental Congress meets in Philadelphia.	17 74	
Fighting breaks out at Lexington and Concord.	17 75	
Thomas Paine publishes *Common Sense.* (Jan.)	17 76	
Congress signs the Declaration of Independence. (July)		
British surrender at Yorktown, Independence is won.	17 81	
	17 89	The French Revolution begins in Paris.
	1790	

Project Progress Report
Plan an Exhibit

Before you begin to assemble your display board, make a plan or model of what you intend to do. This will allow you to make revisions and additions easily, and to see what might be needed to tell your story better.

Here are some pointers:

- Decide on a **focus or main idea** for your exhibit. Center or highlight it on   your board. Maybe you also want to show two sides of something or compare/contrast or before/after, using the two side panels.
- Decide on a **title**. It does NOT have to be the same as your topic. For example, an exhibit about Abraham Lincoln could be titled "The Great Emancipator." (But only if your focus was Lincoln and the slavery issue.)
- Let your **pictures tell the story**. Use maps, charts, graphs, timelines, copies of documents, as well as photographs and illustrations.
- Pay close attention to **story flow**: the reader should not have to jump all over the board to get the story straight. Organize the pieces of your story into a logical, easy to understand layout.
- Work the **theme** in wherever appropriate and effective.
- **Captions** should be in SHORT paragraphs. You are allowed only 500 student-written words on the board, including the title. Don't waste words by repeating information or by stating what is obvious in the picture, map, or document. Instead, tell what it means to your story.
- Don't forget **context**, background and setting. When and where does the story take place? What happened before? What resulted or came after? What was happening in other parts of the country or world at that time? What was the political or social climate?
- Be sure you tell the **whole story**. The reader should not have to know the story to understand your exhibit, nor should supplementary materials be necessary.
- **Color and graphics** should not only fit the topic, but complement it.
- **Legacy** is an important part of every story. And it makes a good conclusion. Tell why your story was important—then? Now? What did it cause? What do we have or do today because of it?

For your PPR grade: Make a scale drawing or fold a sheet of paper into panels to represent a display board. Show as much detail as you can at this time. Your plan will be evaluated on the items above.

 If you want to see good examples of exhibits, visit a local museum and check out how their displays are set up.

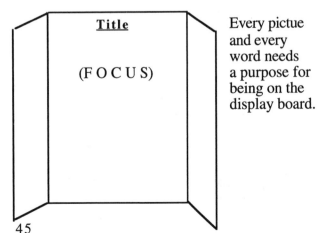

Every pictue and every word needs a purpose for being on the display board.

Project Progress Report
Make an Outline for the Historical Paper

1. Review your notes, also use your timeline if you have one, and decide how you want to tell the story you have researched and taken notes on. You may want to use colored pencils or other ways to sort your notes into groups of similar information.

2. Each group of information will become a Roman Numeral on your outline and later a paragraph in your paper.

3. Give each group/Roman Numeral a title like "Introduction," "Causes," or "Early Career," that tells what that paragraph will be about.

4. Under each Roman Numeral list the details you want to include in the paragraph as "A", "B", "C", etc. Some will need to be broken down further as "1", "2", "3", then "a", "b", "c", and so on.

5. Use as many Roman Numerals as you have material for paragraphs. Paragraph titles and detail titles do not have to be sentences—phrases or just words are better, shorter, easier to understand.

6. Most History Fair Historical Papers need at least ten to fifteen paragraphs. The NHD rules call for 1500 to 2500 words. History Research Papers for class should be _____to_____words.

(Example)
Title of Paper

I. Introduction
    A. Thesis sentence or main idea
    B. Explain relevance to theme
    C. Tell why the topic is important
    D. Set the story in time and place

II. _____
    A. _____
    B. _____
        1. _____
        2. _____
    C. _____

    (and so on)

XX. (or whatever number you get to) Conclusion
    A. Restate importance.
    B. Explain any legacy or something special you have learned.
    C. Restate connection to History Fair theme.

Topic_____ Name_____ Date_____ Class_____

Project Progress Report
Plan a Performance

Decide how you want to tell your story, then make an outline following the format below.
1. TITLE: (if you have one) _____

2. INTRODUCTION: Who does it? _____
                  What does it tell?   A. _____
                                  B. _____
                                  C. _____

3. SCENES:

#____	Setting	Characters	Tells........ (main idea)
#____	Setting	Characters	Tells........ (main idea)
#____	Setting	Characters	Tells........ (main idea)
		(use back if more scenes are needed)	

4. CLOSING: Who? _____Tells: _____

_____

5. PRIMARY SOURCES TO BE QUOTED: _____

6. MAJOR PROPS NEEDED: _____

47

Topic_____ Name_____ Date_____ Class_____

Make a Documentary Storyboard

Decide how you want to present your story: What order, which pictures you want to use, and what each tells. Then fill out the diagram below.

1. Title: _____

2. Introduction:

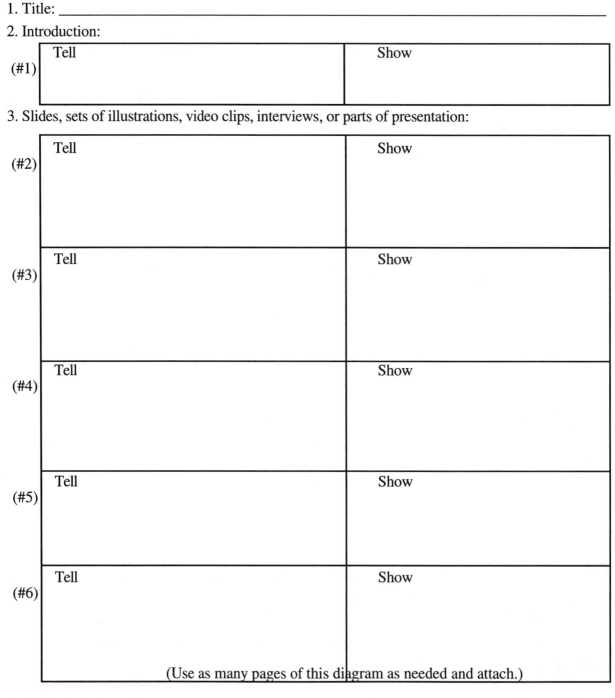

	Tell	Show
(#1)		

3. Slides, sets of illustrations, video clips, interviews, or parts of presentation:

	Tell	Show
(#2)		
(#3)		
(#4)		
(#5)		
(#6)		

(Use as many pages of this diagram as needed and attach.)

4. To include in credits: _____

Research Skills Test

I. Vocabulary: In the paragraph below study the sentences for meaning, then fill in the blanks with vocabulary terms from the lists at the right.

Suzie chose to study Harriet Tubman as her_____#1_____ for
a history project. The teacher said to use several different kinds of
information sources   to gather the material she would then combine
into one story for her paper. This process is called_____#2_____.
First, Suzie used a reference book to get background information.
In the library Suzie found a Tubman_____#3_____ which she checked
out to read. She also looked in her American history textbook, using
the ____#4_____ to find the pages where she read about Tubman's
part in the larger story of slavery and the Civil War. On the Internet
she located a(n) ____#5_____ source, a letter written by Tubman to
President Lincoln in 1862.

CHOICES

A. primary
B. index
C. topic
D. biography
E. research

After taking many pages of notes, Suzie was ready to organize
her collected facts into a(n) _____#6_____. Using this plan, she wrote
her rough draft. Several revisions later the paper was ready.   For the
___#7_____ Suzie made a list of the four _____#8_____ she had used,
arranging them in ____#9_____order by the ____#10___'s last name.
Now her paper was ready to turn in.

A. outline
B. alphabetical
C. sources
D. author
E. bibliography

II. Bibliographic Form: Imagine you use a book called *A Dozen American Lives* by John
Planter. It was published in Chicago, in 1996, by the Young Reader's Guild Press. Please
arrange the information **as you would for your bibliography** by answering "**A**" for the
part that goes first, "**B**" for the next part, "**C**" for the part that follows, then "**D,**" and "**E**"
for the part that comes last.

_____ 11. Chicago

_____ 12. Young Reader's Guild Press

_____ 13. John Planter (Planter, John)

_____ 14. 1996

_____ 15. *A Dozen American Lives*

III. Subtopics and Related Topics: Match the topic list on the left to the "subtopics" or "related" topics on the right. Write the letter in the blank by the number. Match evenly. **Use each answer only once.**

_____16. Pilgrims   **A.** locomotives

_____17. Abraham Lincoln   **B.** Mexico

_____18. the First Railroad   **C.** Religious freedom

_____19. Martin Luther King, Jr.   **D.** Civil War

_____20. Spanish Colonies   **E.** the Civil Rights Movement

IV. Locating Information: Below is a list of some well-known reference works. Which one would be the best to find the answers for the questions that follow? Write the letter of your choice in the blank to the left. **Use each answer as often as needed.**

A. *Documents of American History*   **D.** *Webster's Student Dictionary*
B. *Notable American Women*   **E.** *Rand McNally Historical Atlas*
C. *Bartlett's Quotations*   *of the World*

_____ 21. Who said "I have not yet begun to fight!"?

_____ 22. Which parts of Europe were once part of the Roman Empire?

_____ 23. When and where did Amelia Earhart fly her first plane?

_____ 24. What rights did Jefferson list in the Declaration of Independence?

_____ 25. Where was the Battle of Gettysburg?

_____ 26. Did the 1863 Emancipation Proclamation free all slaves?

_____ 27. What is the difference between "biography" and "bibliography"?

_____ 28. How old was Clara Barton when she founded the American Red Cross?

_____ 29. What do the terms "Middle Ages" and "Renaissance" really mean?

_____ 30. How large was Texas when it was a republic?

V. Your Topic: Answer the questions below based on your own research.

1. Who or what are you researching? _____

2. What happened? or what was accomplished?_____

_____

_____

3. When and where does your story take place? _____

_____

4. Why is this story important? _____

_____

_____

5. How can we see the results or legacy today? _____

_____

_____

6. How do we know about this person or event? _____

_____

_____

7. Briefly explain the main points of your story in your own words.

_____

_____

_____

_____

_____

_____

_____

_____

_____

_____

_____

_____

History Fair
Exhibit Evaluation

Title: _____

Students: 1._____ 2._____
3._____ 4._____
5._____

I. Research and Historical Quality (60 pts.)
(15) A. Complete story on board _____
(15) B. Clearly demonstrates theme _____
(10) C. Correct facts _____
(10) D. Choice of illustrations _____
(10) E. Use of sources, including primary
sources, if available. _____   Subtotal: _____
Comments: _____
_____

II. Required Paperwork (20 pts.)
(10) A. Process Narrative (theme, choice of topic,
analysis, development) _____
(10) B. Annotated Bibliography (sources, form,
primary sources, annotations) _____   Subtotal: _____
Comments: _____
_____

III. Overall Presentation (20 pts.)
(5) A. Logical layout, focus _____
(5) B. Efficient use of space _____
(5) C. Neat and attractive; captions typed _____
(5) D. Grammar and spelling (titles, captions) _____   Subtotal: _____

Comments: _____
_____

IV. Penalties:
___ size/word limits   ___ spelling/grammar
___ names on project   ___ items not typed
___ text not clear   ___ encyclopedia cited
___ messy   ___ Other: _____   Penalty: - _____

V. Extra Credit
For: _____   Bonus: + _____
_____

PROJECT GRADE TOTAL: _____

History Fair
Paper Evaluation

Title: _____

Student: _____ **Topic:** _____

I. Research and Historical Quality (60 pts.)
    (15) A. Correct facts/complete story   _____

    (15) B. Shows historical significance of topic   _____

    (10) C. Clearly demonstrates theme   _____

    (10) D. Demonstrates analysis and interpretation   _____

    (10) E. Uses sources appropriately, including

              primary sources, if available.   _____   Subtotal: _____

    Comments: _____

    _____

II. Bibliography (15 pts.)
    (5) A. Annotations appropriate   _____

    (5) B. Sources balanced and varied   _____

    (5) C. Follows rules and uses proper form   _____   Subtotal: _____

    Comments: _____

    _____

III. Overall Presentation (25 pts.)
    (5) A. Logical organization   _____

    (5) B. Introduction and Conclusion   _____

    (5) C. Appropriate use of quotations   _____

    (5) D. Neat and attractive   _____

    (5) E. Grammar and spelling   _____   Subtotal: _____

    Comments: _____

    _____

IV. Penalties:
    ___ length/word limits   ___ spelling/grammar

    ___ title page incorrect   ___ paper not typed

    ___ not historically accurate   ___ encyclopedia cited

    ___ source citations   ___ Other:_____   Penalty: - _____

    Comments: _____

V. Extra Credit
    For: _____   Bonus: + _____

    _____

PROJECT GRADE TOTAL: _____

Performance Evaluation

Title: _____

Students: 1._____   2._____

3._____   4._____

5._____

I. Research and Historical Quality (60 pts.)

(20) A. Story complete in presentation   _____

(20) B. Clearly demonstrates theme   _____

(10) C. Places story in historical context
and shows significance   _____

(10) D. Uses available sources appropriately,
including primary sources   _____   Subtotal: _____

Comments: _____

_____

II. Required Paperwork (20 pts.)

(10) A. Process Narrative: theme, choice of topic,
analysis, development   _____

(10) B. Annotated Bibliography: sources, form,
primary sources, annotations   _____   Subtotal: _____

Comments: _____

_____

III. Overall Presentation (20 pts.)

(5) A. Logical story flow, scene sequence   _____

(5) B. Efficient use of time   _____

(5) C. Stage presence, voice quality   _____

(5) D. Appropriate costumes and props   _____   Subtotal: _____

Comments: _____

_____

IV. Penalties:

___ time limit   ___ dialogue/lines

___ no introduction   ___ not historically accurate

___ grammar/spelling   ___ paperwork not typed

___ awkward scene   ___ Other: _____   Penalty: - _____
change(s)

V. Extra Credit:

For: _____   Bonus: + _____

_____

PROJECT GRADE TOTAL: _____

History Fair
Documentary Evaluation

Title: _____

Students: 1._____   2._____
               3._____   4._____
               5._____

I. Research and Historical Quality (60 pts.)
     (20) A. Story complete in presentation   _____
     (20) B. Clearly demonstrates theme   _____
     (10) C. Places story in historical context and
            shows significance   _____
     (10) D. Uses available sources appropriately,
            including primary sources   _____   Subtotal: _____
     Comments: _____

_____

II. Required Paperwork (20 pts.)
     (10) A. Process Narrative: theme, choice of topic,
            analysis, development   _____
     (10) B. Annotated Bibliography: sources, form,
            primary sources, annotations   _____   Subtotal: _____
     Comments: _____

_____

III. Overall Presentation (20 pts.)
     (5) A. Logical story flow, illustration sequence   _____
     (5) B. Efficient use of time   _____
     (5) C. Appropriate script, music   _____
     (5) D. Visual impact   _____   Subtotal: _____
     Comments: _____

_____

IV. Penalties:
     ___ time limit   ___ not student narrated
     ___ no introduction   ___ not historically accurate
     ___ grammar/spelling   ___ papers not typed
     ___ equipment not   ___ no credits given
          student operated   ___ Other: _____   Penalty: - _____

V. Extra Credit:
     For: _____   Bonus: + _____

_____

PROJECT GRADE TOTAL: _____

Research Paper Evaluation

Student:_____ Date:_____

Topic/Title: _____

I. RULES and FORM (20 points)
A. Cover _____
B. Title Page (title, name, class, date) _____
C. Outline (corrected and recopied) _____
D. Paper   1. length (3-5 pages) _____
           2. introduction _____
           3. conclusion _____
E. Bibliography
           1. variety of sources, 3 minimum _____
           2. proper bibliographic form _____   **Part I.**_____

II. HISTORICAL CONTENT (60 points)
A. Correct Facts _____
B. Evidence of Research _____
C. Story Complete _____
D. Told in Logical Sequence _____

    *Extra Credit: Shows understanding and insight of topic _____ **Part II.**_____

III. PRESENTATION (20 points)
A. Neat and Attractive: typed or written in ink _____
B. Easy to Read   1. clear and complete thoughts _____
               2. organized paragraphs _____
               3. spelling _____
               4. grammar and punctuation _____
               5. elaborative detail _____   **Part III.**_____

IV. EXTRA CREDIT and PENALTIES

A. Early completion	_____	F. Extra sources	_____
B. Typed	_____	G. Late	_____
C. Illustrations	_____	H. Messy	_____
D. Decorated cover	_____	I. Incomplete	_____
E. Primary sources	_____	J. More than one encyclopedia	_____

Part IV._____

TOTAL SCORE: _____

Topic _____ Name _____ Date _____ Class _____

Project Progress Report
Debrief the Project

1. Title: _____ Category _____

   Group or Individual? _____ Did you place? _____

2. What was the most valuable or useful thing you learned **how to do** while working on this project?

_____

_____

_____

3. What was the most interesting fact you learned **about your topic**? How did it   change your understanding of the topic's **importance in history**?

_____

_____

_____

_____

_____

4. What are you **most proud of** doing or learning in this project?

_____

_____

_____

5. What would you **change or do differently** if you could start over?

_____

_____

_____

IV. Student Research and Presentation

How to Use the Items in This Section

For the Classroom Teacher

The classroom teacher or fair director can use any combination of the handouts in this section for student information packets. Some are general suggestions or skill lessons while others are designed for specific situations in research or project development. No teacher is expected to use all the items included, but having a wide selection of simple "how-to" forms makes the time spent coaching student researchers more efficient and effective.

For the Parent or Student

The History Fair parent will find the handouts in this section very useful as guides and checklists. As your student progresses through the various stages of research and project preparation, specific instructions are sometimes necessary. Often parents want to advise, but are not sure of contest expectations and requirements. All of these handouts were designed both to teach the skills needed and to serve as instructions for the different parts of the project according to National History Day rules. The parent can help the student apply the ideas and suggestions to his or her own topic and presentation.

In This Section

Student Timeline is a calendar-chart listing the various parts of the project with suggested time frames and spaces for due dates for assignments. Time management is probably the hardest part of a major project like History Fair for a middle school student to learn. This form shows the student steps for the whole project and allows the student to easily plan work .

Getting the Details is a simple how-to list for taking good notes. Students may take their notes either on traditional note cards or on regular notebook paper.

Primary vs. Secondary Sources is a T-chart explanation of the two types of information and how to find them. Most students need frequent reminders of what the difference is. (Be sure they get over the notion that a "primary source" is the one used most.) Note: The criteria for what constitutes a primary source are somewhat relaxed for History Fair participation to include items in translation and published collections.

Make a Bibliography gives rules for compiling and writing a standard bibliography and gives examples of various types of sources. **The Annotated Bibliography** gives rules and suggestions for listing and annotating different types of sources according to National History Day guidelines.

Interviews and Oral Histories gives suggestions on how to plan, conduct, and use an interview or recorded oral history. Some topics suggest oral histories more than others, but this is always an exciting and unusual way to research.

The **Interview Release Agreement** and **Receipt for Borrowed Item** are short forms for the student to use when interviewing an expert or recording an oral history. The **Receipt** form can also be used when students borrow books, artifacts, or equipment from private sources, or items to be used as props or costumes in performances from friends, neighbors, or family.

Helpful Hints for Winning Projects is a list of suggestions for all projects, especially those going on to advanced competition.

Hints for **Exhibits**, **Papers**, **Performances**, and **Documentaries** give specific suggestions for the category addressed. Most ideas are common sense, but easily overlooked by students. These handouts can be used like checklists.

61

Historical Paper Checklist is useful not only for the Historical Papers category, but also for the Process Narrative or the class research paper.

Don't Forget the Paperwork gives a suggested outline of the Process Narrative and a summary of rules for the Annotated Bibliography. (Examples can be found in the handout **Make a Bibliography/The Annotated Bibliography** described above.) All projects except Papers must include a Process Narrative.

Interview Dos and Don'ts is helpful for students who enter the Performance or Documentary categories since they must be interviewed by the judges beginning at the campus fair. Other category winners will have interviews at advanced levels of competition. Sometimes the interview is the determining factor in the judges' choice of winners, so be sure to prepare for a good impression.

Student Timeline

Dates	Activity	PPRs Due
(1 week min.)	**TOPIC:** • Choose topic, read general background information • Gather, read, take notes from secondary sources • Look for primary sources	# ___ _____ # ___ _____ Last day to change topic: _____
(2-4 weeks)	**RESEARCH, RESEARCH, RESEARCH** • Visit area libraries, museums; make calls for interviews • Evaluate primary sources • Gather pictures, quotes, etc., to use in presentation • Computer lab or home Internet searches	# ___ _____ # ___ _____ # ___ _____ # ___ _____
(1 week or less)	**ORGANIZE** • Decide how you want to tell your story • Make an outline of the project • Fill in gaps with more research • Evaluate materials and decide on category • Begin planning scripts or board layout	# ___ _____ # ___ _____ # ___ _____ Last day to change category: _____
(1-2 weeks)	**CREATE PROJECT PRESENTATION** **Exhibit** •gather materials •make letters for titles and subtitles •copy photos; create illustrations •write, type, trim captions •word count; check spelling and grammar •mat and mount everything •models, artifacts? **Performance** •write script •memorize lines and practice •practice, practice, practice •gather props; make backdrops •decide on costumes •practice and more practice •perform for family, friends, class **Documentary** •take pictures; shoot video; scan images •write script; match with visuals •revise and edit •check time •add music, titles, credits **Paper** •write rough draft •edit, revise, and improve •word count •check spelling and grammar •check references/sources •have paper checked by an English teacher	# ___ _____ # ___ _____ # ___ _____ # ___ _____ # ___ _____
(1 week or less)	**PAPERWORK** • Bibliography—separate primary and secondary sources. Write annotations, alphabetize, and type. • Process Narrative (not required for Paper category)— Write rough draft; revise and edit; check word count. Have all papers read by an English teacher.	# ___ _____ # ___ _____
(1-2 days)	**BE READY ON TIME** • Double-check everything; do things you forgot. • Extra copies of paperwork—plain title page, no names	**Campus History Fair date:** _____

Getting the Details
How to Take Good Notes

1. Use the index to locate information more quickly.

2. Develop a standard method of writing information. Always put the bibliographic facts from the source you are using at the top of the page or card. On the second and following pages/cards of notes from the same source you may use the last name of the author only—always with the page number.

3. Put the number of the page you are using in the margin beside your notes from that page.

4. Read at least one or two paragraphs before taking any notes—*read for the sense* of the passage. Then start taking notes: read—take notes, read—take notes, etc. (Alternate processes.)

5. Give your notes a general title. (You can do this last if it's easier for you, but it makes sorting the notes into "parts of the story" much quicker.)

6. Use phrases or words to take down the important information, main ideas, and details you want to remember.

7. Carefully copy names, dates, other details that you may wish to use so you do not have to double-check them later.

8. Always put quotes ("xxxxx") around anything you copy word-for-word. And make sure you have the correct page number. If you use this quote, or the main idea of it, you must cite the source exactly, that is, tell where it came from. Failure to do this is plagiarism.

9. Number your pages of notes and keep all your notes together in a folder or notebook that you bring to class everyday (or a "pack" of note cards).

10. Keep all your notes until after the project is complete, turned in, graded, and returned.

Primary vs. Secondary Sources

History Fair rules require the use of primary sources if they are available. Many are. Here is the difference between Primary and Secondary sources:

Primary

- Created at the time the event being studied occurred.

- Or created by a participant of the event being studied.

- **Examples:** letters, diaries, and journals, also flight records or ship's logs; business records; government documents; photographs and films; audio tapes; oral history interviews with people who were involved in or witnessed the event being studied; newspaper or magazine articles from the time of the event being studied; songs, poems, ads; autobiographies

- Is the "raw" material—you have to figure out what it means to your topic and what is important about it.

- Can easily be biased—so examine the source carefully. Some questions to ask:
  1. Why was this item created?
  2. Was the creator promoting a particular viewpoint?
  3. Does it contradict information from other sources?

Secondary*

- Created at any time after the event being studied occurred.

- Created by a third party like an historian, a film maker, or a writer.

- **Examples:** encyclopedias and other reference books or sets of books; history textbooks; documentaries (the "original film" included is primary); interviews with "experts" on the event being studied such as a college professor or a museum curator; newspaper or magazine articles written at a later time; worksheets, handouts, or "lessons" about the event; biographies

- Is the "processed information". Someone else has read the primary sources and decided what they mean. The historian tells you what happened and why it is important.

- Can be biased, also. Check credentials of the writer or creator.

* Reliable, unbiased, secondary sources can usually be found in school, public, and university libraries.

Where to find Primary Sources:
- Most textbooks have "readings" in the back. Check yours to see if it includes an item related to the event you are studying.
- Your teacher or library may have "source books" or primary source collections.
- Museums and historical society libraries are full of primary sources.
- Government records—city, county, state and federal. Most are open to the public if you ask.
- Some may be found on the Internet, but make sure they are authentic. (Stick to established, reliable sites like the Smithsonian Institution or the National Archives.)
- Check the bibliographies in the secondary sources you use to see what primary sources that author used to research the subject.
- Family and/or friends may have items you can use. Ask!

Make a Bibliography

I. General Rules
- Use standard and consistent form. See the examples below.
- Make sure your information is complete and correct.
- Include every source you used for information or for illustration.
- Alphabetize by the first word in the entry: author's last name, first word of title, and so on.
- Make a separate page at the end of your paper and title it "Bibliography."
- List all your sources in alphabetical order. Do NOT indent the first line, but DO INDENT the second and all following lines, if it goes past one line. Skip a line between entries.
- List specific page numbers at the end if you read only a few pages of the book.
- Do NOT number your entries.

II. Examples
encyclopedia with author
Upjohn, Everard. "Architecture." <u>Encyclopedia Americana</u>, Vol. 2. Danbury: Grolier Inc., 1994, pp. 149-152.

encyclopedia with no author
"Abraham Lincoln." <u>Collier's Encyclopedia</u>, Vol. 8. New York: Collier, 1995, pp. 281-283.

book with one author
Reef, Catherine. <u>Civil War Soldiers</u>. New York: Henry Holt and Company, 1993.

book with two authors
Freedman, Lawrence, and Efrain Karsh. <u>The Gulf Conflict 1990-1991</u>. Princeton: Princeton University Press, 1993.

book with more than two authors
Quirk, Randolph, and others. <u>A Comprehensive Grammar of the English Language</u>. London: Longman Publications, 1984.

magazine article
Murphy, Cullen. "Women and the Bible." <u>Atlantic Monthly</u>. August, 1993, pp. 39-64.

newspaper article
Feder, Barnaby J. "For Job Seekers, a Toll-Free Gift of Expert Advice." <u>New York Times</u>. Dec. 30, 1993, p. D1.

video/movie
"Hearts and Hands." from The American Experience series. Public Broadcasting Service, 1992.

interview
Jackson, John H. Personal interview. San Antonio, Texas, September 9, 1997.

e-mail
Smulyan, Susan. "Sewing machine company trade cards." Personal e-mail, September 14, 1998.

website
"Who Invented the Cotton Gin?" Whole Cloth: Discovering Science and Technology through American Textile History. National Museum of American History, Smithsonian Institution. <http://www.si.edu/lemelson/centerpieces/whole_cloth> (Sept. 14, 2000).

For History Fair Projects

The Annotated Bibliography

- All projects must have an annotated bibliography of five or more sources. Do not list the encyclopedias you used for general background information.

- At least two sources should be "primary" if at all possible.

- Use standard bibliographic form for all information from each source.

- Separate primary from secondary sources. List the primary sources first, then the secondary sources, each list should be in alphabetic order.

- Annotations are brief descriptions of the sources and how each was used in the development of the project.

- Annotations for primary sources should explain why the source is primary for your topic.

Examples of Annotations

Primary

Foner, Phillip. The Factory Girls. Chicago: University of Illinois Press, 1977.

This collection of documents tells of the struggle for shorter working days and better working conditions which eventually brought about the beginning of the first trade unions of women workers in the United States.

The Queen of Fashion Monthly. Vol. XIX, No. 11. New York: July, 1892.

This 1892 fashion magazine provided pictures of tailor-made gowns of the latest style. There are also a number of advertisements for sewing machines throughout the magazine showing models and prices.

Secondary

Bettmann, Otto L. The Good Old Days: They Were Terrible. New York: Random House, 1974.

Sewers for the garment industry often worked in sweatshops. Most workers were women, children and immigrants. Each worker had a set quota and most worked eighty-four-hour weeks at a wage averaging five cents an hour.

Paradis, Adrian. The Labor Reference Book. Philadelphia: Chilton Book Company, 1972.

A very extensive reference which details how the International Ladies' Garment Workers' Union was formed in 1900. This was the first union to offer six-day work weeks, ten holidays per year, and workers would be paid immediately instead of having to wait for garments to be sold.

Interviews and Oral Histories

I. Before the Interview
- Do your homework: learn as much as possible about the person to be interviewed and/or the topic(s) for discussion.
- Prepare a list of open-ended, "how" or "why" questions. Don't use questions that suggest how the person should respond. Write the questions down.
- Pack a tape recorder, several blank tapes, microphone, extension cord or extra batteries, a notebook and the questions. Practice using the equipment.
- If you are concerned about technique, practice with parents or another adult.

II. At the Interview
- Begin the recording with names, topic, date and place.
- Take careful notes on specific dates, names, places, or unfamiliar words, to get them exact and spelled correctly.
- Be flexible. The prepared questions are only a guide. Allow the interviewee to elaborate or add things.
- Ask only one question at a time, and allow the person time to answer completely.
- It may be appropriate to ask for an opinion or to confirm connections in the story.
- Always ask for additional comments before quitting. Also, check for availability of documents or artifacts to examine, photograph, or borrow.

III. After the Interview
- Label all tapes and punch-out tabs on cassettes so the interview won't be accidentally erased or taped over.
- Write a thank-you note and send to the interviewee.

IV. Oral Histories
- It is a good idea to transcribe the recording of the interview and send a copy to the interviewee for validation. Edit out extra, unnecessary words and phrases or repetitions to make it easier to read.
- Have the interviewee "sign off" on a copy of the interview. That is, give you written permission to use his or her story in your History Fair project.
- Be sure to compare "facts" given in an oral history with other sources before accepting them as historical truth. Remember, beliefs and time sometimes color people's memory.
- Continue research in other primary and secondary sources. Don't base the entire project on one source, no matter how interesting or compelling.

V. Uses for Oral Histories
- Present various points of view.
- Document unusual skills or crafts.
- Gather details about an event from a participant or eyewitness.
- Demonstrate the character of an individual.
- Explain motivations or changes of opinion.
- Help construct a sequence of events or establish the setting of a story.

Interview Release Agreement

I, _____, have been interviewed this

date _____ by _____ who is a student

at _____ school. I understand that he/she

will use my interview for his/her History Fair project titled (or about)

_____;

and that no other use will be made of my oral memoir unless I give specific

permission.

_____   _____
                (interviewee)   (date)

_____   _____
         (student interviewer)   (date)

(Make a copy of this agreement for each person involved)

Receipt for Borrowed Item

Lender: _____ Phone: _____

    Address: _____

Borrower: _____ Phone: _____

    Address: _____

Item(s) borrowed: _____

_____

_____

Conditions: To be used in the creation of a History Fair project in the following way(s).

_____

_____

_____

Item(s) to be returned on or before _____.

_____   _____
(student borrower)   (date)

_____   _____
(lender)   (date)

(Make a copy for each person involved)

Helpful Hints for Winning Projects
General Suggestions for All Categories

- A winning project will touch an emotion—hope, despair, humor, anger, etc. The goal is to make the judge laugh, or cry, or get mad when he or she views the project.

- Keep it simple and focused. Don't try to include everything. A good project is a distillation of research.

- Choose an interesting topic—something unusual, rather than the usual. Winners are often local or family history (primary sources are available and are easily accessible.) Always place local history topics in national or international context. If the project teaches the judge something, it is already ahead of the competition.

- Never assume the judge will make the connection between the project topic and the theme. State the obvious—anywhere it is appropriate.

- Since "historical quality" is 60 percent of the score, concentrate on good solid research and analysis rather than a flashy presentation or technique.

- Use interviews—if "primary sources" are unavailable for interview, try contacting experts like college professors, community leaders, or museum curators.

- Old newspapers are an excellent source of primary information—even the ads.

- Use a number of different types of sources. Visit the school library, a university or public library, a museum, conduct an interview, watch a documentary, or use the Internet.

- Let the topic and the research determine the category to enter.
    - Lots of written primary sources—paper or performance
    - Lots of primary source photos or copies of documents—exhibit
    - No primary sources, but pictures in books and on the Internet—documentary
    - No primary source hard copy or photos in books—performance

- Keep good research notes, and compile the bibliography very carefully. Bibliography should use standard form, either MLA or Turabian. When in doubt as to how to cite a source, look it up or ask a librarian. Be consistent. Always have your paperwork proofed by an English teacher. Always keep one copy of everything for yourself.

- Always write the one-to-two-page description (Process Narrative) last, after the project is complete and there is time to reflect on what was learned.

- Use the judges' critique(s) to revise and improve after every level of competition. Expand topic research and the bibliography.

Hints for Exhibits
Ideas Every Exhibit Should Consider

- After most of the research has been done, visit a museum to see how a professional exhibit looks and how it is organized.

- The focus or main idea needs to be centered and obvious, possibly something clever or unusual.

- A catchy title is always a plus, maybe play on a quote or saying, or the theme.

- The topic may need to be defined. Try showing both sides of an issue or story.

- The exhibit should stand alone. Should not need supplementary materials or student explanation for the judge, or anyone, to understand it.

- Be sure the sequence and/or layout makes sense. Group parts of your story. Don't glue things permanently to the board; allow for possible changes.

- Tell the story in pictures with as few words as possible. The rules allow you 500 words, 300 is better. Write what you want to say first, cut and edit later.

- Timelines are a good way to show incidents in an event or to demonstrate cause and effect; likewise for charts and graphs. Check out the graphics on CNN or in the Sunday newspaper for ideas.

- All written material—especially captions—should be proofed by an English teacher (for grammar and spelling) AND by a history teacher (for accuracy).

- Color is a powerful tool, use it appropriately and sparingly. Limit colors used to two or three. Stay away from patterns if there are lots of pictures.

- Backboard should be covered, painted, or made from some attractive material. (Bargain fabrics can be found in any large fabric store.)

- Lettering should be impressive and look professional, even unusual, if appropriate. Adhesives should never show. All illustrations should have mats. Edges of the board should be covered.

- Use a drop cloth (maybe in fabric matching the board?) under the project to define the space and make any items placed in front stand out.

- Copied pictures can be hand colored with map pencils. Pictures can be mounted on cardboard to stand up, or stand out from the board, for a 3-D effect.

- Make it eye-catching—something that says "Look at me!" Try an odd-shaped board, 3-D cutouts or stand-ups, a model combined with a poster, a surprise ending, or doors that open, or be creative. What will best enhance the project and topic?

- DON'T CLUTTER!!

Hints for Historical Papers

- The basics count. A good thesis statement and a thorough outline make a big difference. Clarity in writing begins with a carefully considered plan.

- Read examples of previous National History Day winning papers in the *Junior Historian* magazine.

- Put extra thought into your introduction, since it sets the stage, and into your conclusion because it makes a lasting impression.

- Make sure you show how your story fits into the "big picture" of history, and how it has remained important over time.

- Use quotes from oral histories or primary sources whenever appropriate. Also, conclusions you make based on your interpretation of primary sources are more persuasive and interesting than a compilation of opinions from secondary sources.

- Be sure to credit every direct quote and idea not your own. (Failure to do this is plagiarism.) Decide whether to use footnotes or end notes, then get a style manual and follow the instructions exactly. Sometimes English teachers or librarians have handouts on this procedure.

- Remember, a good historical paper is an analysis and interpretation of events, not just a report. Don't be afraid to take a position as long as you support it with facts and quotes from your research.

- Do not write yourself into the paper. You may, however, write yourself into the annotations in the bibliography.

- A paper is to be read. It should inform and entertain, even challenge the reader. Be sure to read your draft aloud before making the final version.

- Work in the theme—or the theme vocabulary—whenever you can.

- Have your paper read by both an English teacher (for grammar and style) and a history teacher (for accuracy) before you do the final draft.

- You may incorporate illustrations into the body of your paper and/or add supplementary materials at the end. In both cases, be very selective! Use only items that truly add to your story.

- Get rid of as many *to be* verbs as possible (is, are, were, was, will be, have been, etc.). Replace them with action verbs if you can.

- Use a simple, plain font with print no larger than 12 pt. Use standard white paper, double-space, and 1" margins all around. Number pages, staple upper left corner. Title page should only have title, category, and entry number. (No names at the campus fair.) No decoration or additional cover of any kind.

Hints for Performances

Steps to Follow

1. Decide how to tell the story. Write a rough draft or outline of the script. Locate primary sources that can be quoted as part of the dialogue.

2. Write the script. Remember the time limit is ten minutes. Be sure to allow a few seconds for unplanned pauses or forgotten lines. (Exceeding the ten minute time limit can result in the project being disqualified.)

3. Have the script edited by both an English teacher and a history teacher.

4. Memorize lines.

5. Make a list of costumes, props, and backdrops to be used. Start collecting them. (Local high school drama departments or community theaters may be willing to lend some items.)

6. Practice using all props. Practice it until it can be presented cold. Then, practice in front of an audience. Add music, lights, special effects, if they add to the total presentation.

7. Get critiques from practice audiences and perfect the performance.

8. Assemble the Annotated Bibliography and the Process Narrative. (Save everything on both disk and hard drive.) Have extra copies ready on the day of the performance.

Some Practical Advice

1. Keep props, costumes, and backdrops simple. Only five minutes are allowed to set up and another five to take down. Also, the project might win, and have to be transported to another location or another city. Most important, the student presenters are the stars, not the "stuff."

2. It is not necessary to spend a lot of money on costumes or props. Look for items at thrift stores and junk shops. Ask family and neighbors. (Some people have amazing collections in their attics or storerooms!)

3. Incorporate primary sources into the script and props whenever appropriate. Even little things, like advertising or popular songs, really give the piece authenticity.

4. Make sure group members can work together. If the group is always fighting, the project will never get done. Make sure all members contribute and work.

5. PRACTICE, PRACTICE, PRACTICE.

6. Go to the History Fair and have fun!

Hints for Documentaries

- Before starting, watch documentaries on the History Channel, PBS, or the Discovery Channel to get an idea of how professional documentaries look and sound.

- Choose a topic that lends itself to visual presentation. During research, collect a variety of visual images—illustrations, artwork, graphics, documents, maps, etc. Keep precise records of where each came from and cite them in the bibliography.

- Use the simplest technology possible to achieve the desired result. Don't be tempted by glitz or exotic techniques. The best documentaries are well researched and presented clearly.

- Outline the script first to tell the story. Time it and edit, if necessary. Then decide on illustrations and synchronize. Add music and/or sound effects to "set the stage" with an emotion or historical time period, but make sure it's not too loud or distracting.

- Timing is essential. Try for a new image about every six to ten seconds. Always time the presentation very carefully and leave at least ten to fifteen seconds leeway.

- Students should not "perform" in a video project, but all voice narration, except for interview or original film clips, should be student voices.

- Keep words on the screen to a minimum. Pictures are much more interesting.

- Students may use either school equipment or their own equipment to produce the project, but all equipment must be student operated. For assistance check with district high schools, local college, or university media department, or a cable access station.

- Do not use more than one minute of preexisting or professional film footage, less is better. And remember, just because the film has sound doesn't mean it must be used. Students may "voice over" and use the film only as illustration for the script, if they wish.

- Clear focus and understandable narration are crucial. Avoid using blurry pictures, no matter how appropriate they are. They will look worse on a large screen.

- When filming an interview, use good lighting and watch for distracting backgrounds or other items that might take away from the interviewee. Have questions prepared in advance. Try not to have "yes" or "no" questions—concentrate on "why" and "how."

- Practice setting up and using the equipment in several locations to make sure it can be done smoothly.

- When competition day arrives, take extra copies of the project (video tape, CD, etc.) and an extension cord, extra light bulb, or replacement for anything that might break, JUST IN CASE.

Historical Paper Checklist

____1. The introduction sets the story in time and place, and tells why the topic is important.

____2. The conclusion gives a summary of the story and states its importance and/or influence in history.

____3. The story flows logically from one paragraph to the next.

____4. The paper is not just a chronology or timeline put into paragraphs.

____5. There are separate paragraphs for each part of the story.

____6. All statements of opinion are supported with a fact or a quote.

____7. All quotes and illustrations are attributed properly with author and page. Then sources are listed completely and described in the Annotated Bibliography.

____8. All proper names are capitalized (people, places, events, etc.).

____9. All pronouns (it, he, they, her, etc.) have clear antecedents, that is, it is clear and obvious who or what the pronoun stands for.

____10. There are no "on-and-on-and-on-and-on" sentences.

____11. Every sentence makes sense (read it out loud—preferably to someone).

____12. All needless words, slang words or phrases, and contractions (didn't, they'll, it's, etc.) have been removed or replaced.

____13. All questionable words have been checked for spelling and/or meaning.

____14. Eliminate words or phrases you do not understand.

____15. The final paper has been through several drafts in order to make it the best possible.

____16. Count words: minimum is 1500, limit is 2500, not counting the Annotated Bibliography. This is approximately six to ten pages typed, double-spaced. Edit or elaborate, if needed.

____17. Type size is no larger that 12 pt., no smaller than 10 pt., and the font is simple, easy to read. Title page has only title, category, and entry number. (No names at the campus fair, no school names at advanced competition.)

Don't Forget the Paperwork

I. Title Page: Plain white paper, no decoration or cover of any kind. Information to include: Name (except at campus History Fair), Title, Category, and project number. Staple in upper left-hand corner.

II. The Process Narrative
1. The official rules say "a one to two page description of how the project was developed." Word limit is 500 words.
2. This is a general guide:

    Title: Use the title of the project (**not** "Process Narrative").

    Introduction: Set the topic in time, explain (briefly) what it is or what happened, and tell why it is important. This is sometimes called an "impact statement" and could also appear on an exhibit board right after the title. Use theme vocabulary if possible.

    Body: • Explain how the topic/project relates to the theme:
    "_____"
    • Should be several paragraphs.
    • Explain why the topic was chosen (personal interests, available primary sources, etc.).
    • Describe how the project was developed—what was actually done, any special circumstances or problems?
    • Elaborate on any unusual or special sources.

    Conclusion: Sum up what has been done, restate relationship to theme and/or significance in history.

III. The Annotated Bibliography
1. All projects must have an annotated bibliography of five or more sources. At least two sources should be primary. Do not include encyclopedias used for general information.

2. Standard (and consistent) form should be used for all bibliographic information. See a style manual or your English teacher for help with unusual sources.

3. Primary sources should be labeled and listed first, in alphabetical order. Then the secondary sources, also in alphabetical order. Do not number.

4. Annotations should give a brief description of the source and tell how it was used in this project. Primary source annotations should explain why the source is primary for this topic. Annotations should be one to three sentences, two to five lines typed. Very important, extremely useful sources may have more elaborate and lengthy annotations.

IV. Print
All papers should be typed in plain font with print no larger that 12 pt.

The Interview
with
The History Fair Judges

DO

1. Speak up, speak clearly, and smile. Be confident, proud, and happy to be there. This is a great opportunity to show both knowledge and enthusiasm.

2. For groups, take turns answering questions. Judges need to know that all members are knowledgeable on your topic.

3. Work in the theme "_____" whenever possible. They like to know that students are focused.

4. Be prepared to explain any item on the board or in the presentation. No detail is insignificant to some judges.

5. Feel free to add comments or elaborate on something you know a lot about. They like enthusiasm.

6. Feel free to express an opinion about the topic or describe a personal response to something learned. They like analysis and evaluation of topic and personal involvement.

7. Look for an opportunity to get in those details, or that interesting little fact, that was really interesting, but could not fit into the presentation. Judges are impressed with command of detail.

8. Be able to talk about the best sources by name (author and title). Remember, the most important part of the project is the research.

9. Always thank the judges and shake their hands. They are offering their free time without compensation simply because they love history.

DON'T

1. Fidget, walk around, or look at the floor. It distracts from your answers.

2. Chew gum. It's rude.

3. For groups: Don't correct or interrupt each other.

4. Pretend to know something you really don't. Instead, ask the judge to suggest a source or reference.

V. Using the Internet

How to Use the Items in This Section

For the Classroom Teacher

As most schools and many homes are now wired for access to the World Wide Web, more and more students are using this technology for their History Fair research. While the possibilities and opportunities seem fantastic, there are some serious pitfalls. In addition, teachers may find great variety in the skills and experience of the students in any one class. These handouts and worksheets assist both student and teacher to navigate the complexities of this medium. Special emphasis is given to establishing the value and legitimacy of websites. The focus is on finding, evaluating, and using reliable websites with pertinent information.

For the Parent or Student

Although finding information on the Internet may seem easy for those experienced in this medium, there are some issues that can be especially troublesome for students doing History Fair research. Don't believe everything you see until you either know the source or can verify it somewhere else is the general rule. The two pages in this section titled Consider the Source (one a handout and one an activity, or PPR) can guide both the student and the parent in determining validity and value of information.

Many students find the Internet extremely useful for locating illustrations, statistics, and primary sources. Be sure to keep accurate notes as to the source of every item collected. See the Cite the Site handout for putting website information in bibliographic form. One way to limit the credibility problem is to stick to standard, well-known sites like the ones listed in A **Few Favorite Websites**.

Two warnings: Students can get carried away by the great amount of information available on some topics and will need guidance in setting appropriate criteria for their choices. Also, the History Fair requirement of *balanced research* means using a variety of sources, only one of which is the Internet, as well as showing both sides of an issue.

In This Section

Why Students Should Use the Internet for History Fair Research was created for the benefit of both teachers and parents. Students don't have to be convinced.

Teacher Do's and Don'ts gives the teacher or parent some guidelines and suggested procedures for efficient and enjoyable use of the computer lab or home computer.

Just Clicking Around is a simplified how-to handout on using the Internet for those students who have little experience or a reference for the pros.

The **Annotated Webpage** is a labeled diagram of a typical Internet homepage, using the National History Day site. It points out the various components and functions available to the web user.

Consider the Source is an outline for checking the validity and reliability of websites. Ultimately, the student has to decide to accept the information or not, but this checklist is a useful tool in arriving at that decision.

PPR - Consider the Source asks the student to select one website and go through the process of formally evaluating its reliability.

Cite the Site gives general guidelines for website and e-mail bibliographic citation. Students need to get all the information possible when using a website and to remember to date their notes.

A Few Favorite Websites lists URLs (addresses) for some standard national websites, including several that have special National History Day sections. These are always good places to start and students can count on their reliability.

Glossary (for the Internet user) provides definitions for some of the common terms used in and for the Internet.

Why Students Should Use the Internet
for History Fair Research

1. To learn real life skills:
- Learn to use the World Wide Web
- Locate specific information
- Organize search strategy
- Find information on given topics
- Be able to tell what is important, relevant, and reliable

2. To practice critical-thinking skills:
- Decide how to use information
- Evaluate sources
- Analyze for point of view

3. To learn organization of ideas:
- Conduct a logical search
- Create a sequenced presentation
- Classify information
- Analyze information in context

4. To find the most current information:
- Recognize trends in historiography
- Evaluate for relevancy
- Find recently released documents, primary sources, or images

5. To find primary sources or other special information:
- Locate many documents, images, and statistics not found in a school library
- Use indexes, catalogs, and databases
- Visit museum sites and take virtual tours

6. To learn social studies objectives or standards:
- Research skills: gather information from various media
- Evaluate and classify historical or cultural information
- Recognize bias and point of view
- Test information for validity

7. To become better researchers:
- Use new technology
- Work independently
- Research like a professional
- Utilize resources to enhance presentations—cool looking stuff!

Teacher Dos and Don'ts

DOs

1. **Do** check the school's Internet access policy. Discuss appropriate use rules with the class before beginning research.

2. **Do** have Just Clicking Around handouts available, and go over basics for those students who need instruction on Internet use.

3. **Do** teach students to copy from Internet sites and paste into word processing folders or onto disks for editing before printing.

4. **Do** provide students with disks to download information and access to a printer.

5. **Do** allow individual students or project groups to create their own Bookmarks folders in either the classroom or the computer lab.

6. **Do** go over bibliographic citation rules. (See student handout Cite the Site.)

7. **Do** encourage a well-rounded and balanced research strategy. No project should rely on only one kind of source.

8. **Do** watch out for:
   • Conspiracy and Hoax sites: everything from JFK assassination to Roswell, some amusing, others truly dangerous.
   • Useless sites: inaccurate or bogus information.
   • Hate sites: sometimes quite subtle.

9. **Do** work in a room or lab where the teacher can see all the screens in use. Walk around and monitor. (If anything seems illegal or inappropriate, have the student stop using the site and contact the campus or district web technology supervisor.)

10. **Do** become familiar with copyright laws and educate the students.

DON'Ts

1 **Don't** assume that because some of the students know how to use the Internet, all do. There will most likely be all levels of skill and experience in the class, so be prepared for some to work independently and others to need lots of assistance and attention.

2. **Don't** be afraid to try it. Even computer novices can learn along with the kids.

3. **Don't** get mired in the intricacies of electronic citations. Stress consistency and clarity. It's very easy to lose sight of the purpose: to find information on a topic and tell where it came from. (See Cite the Site student handout.)

Just Clicking Around
A Student Guide to Using the Internet

The Browser

A software program called a "browser" is needed to get on the Internet. Netscape and Internet Explorer are the most popular and are used in many schools.

The Address

Once on-line, go directly to the website desired by using the address. It's called a URL or Universal Resource Locator. Addresses look like this:

http://www.HistoryChannel.com or **www.whitehouse.gov**

The **www** stands for World Wide Web and means it is a site you can visit and from which you can get information. The extension **com** or **gov** tells you what kind of organization sponsors the site.

.edu	=	educational organization
.gov	=	government
.mil	=	military
.org	=	private, nonprofit organization
.com	=	commercial (business)
.net	=	network

If an address includes @, it is not a website. It is an e-mail address which is used for correspondence. Some websites include e-mail addresses which can be used for individual questions about the site.

Be very careful to type the address correctly. This is where most mistakes are made. Notice that there are no spaces.

Search Engines

If an address is not known, or just to see what's available on the topic, use a program called a "search engine." At this point a search strategy needs to be planned out. Have a list of key words and phrases, which are different ways researchers can look up information. These are the "related topics" and "subtopics" the librarian and the teacher talk about. For example, when researching Frederick Douglass, the student might also try abolitionists or speeches.

When using a search engine, narrow the search as much as possible so time is not wasted on thousands of useless "hits." (Hits are the matches that the search engine finds when it conducts a search of everything on the web and matches it with what was requested.) However, be careful not to narrow the topic so much that it doesn't get any hits at all! When a list of matches is returned to the screen, the search engine will put the ones it thinks match best first. This isn't always what the researcher wants.

Two popular search engines are **Yahoo!** and **Google**. However, the search engine field is constantly changing. Watch for the new arrivals and try them out. There is great variety, so find the one or two that best fit individual needs.

When checking a number of possible sites, speed up the process by suppressing the images. In Netscape, go to View and click the Show Images button off. Then, when an interesting site is found, and the researcher wants to see the pictures, click the Show Images button on.

Note: Every search engine has its own special features and quirks. Use the Help button each offers to get assistance and explanations.

Hint for finding stuff: Sometimes it helps to enter the topic inside quotation marks.

Bookmarks

Once a useful website is found, "bookmark" it so it can be found again. Pull down the Bookmark menu and choose Add Bookmark. If possible, create a folder for the project and store all bookmarks in it. Other group members can do the same.

It is very easy to keep linking to interesting sites and forget where the good information was found. To avoid getting lost, click on the Back button. It will move backwards through all the sites visited to get there.

To get rid of a bookmark, highlight it, then pull down the Edit menu and click on Delete Bookmark.

Downloading

When usable information is found, "download" (copy) it onto a disk or copy and paste it into a personal folder. It can be edited and printed later from the disk or folder. This way valuable time on-line won't be wasted. Be careful to select only what is pertinent. Some websites contain thousands of pages of information. Students may want to save only text or only pictures. Be careful to save each item with a recognizable file name for easy access.

Citing the Source

Always copy down all available information about each website used, whether for text or for illustrations. These details will be needed for the bibliography. This procedure is the same as when using a book or magazine article. Write down the author, if given, the title(s), and the sponsoring organization, which is like a publisher. Then add two more bits: the URL and the exact date the site was visited. See the student handout titled Cite the Site for how to put this information in the bibliography, but be aware that the rules for this type of citation are subject to revision.

Other Sources

Good History Fair research is done with a wide variety of sources: books, magazine articles, primary sources, interviews, and the Internet. Be sure to explore a variety of sources and make the bibliography balanced. Judges tend to be suspicious of research done entirely from one type of source.

A Typical Website Homepage

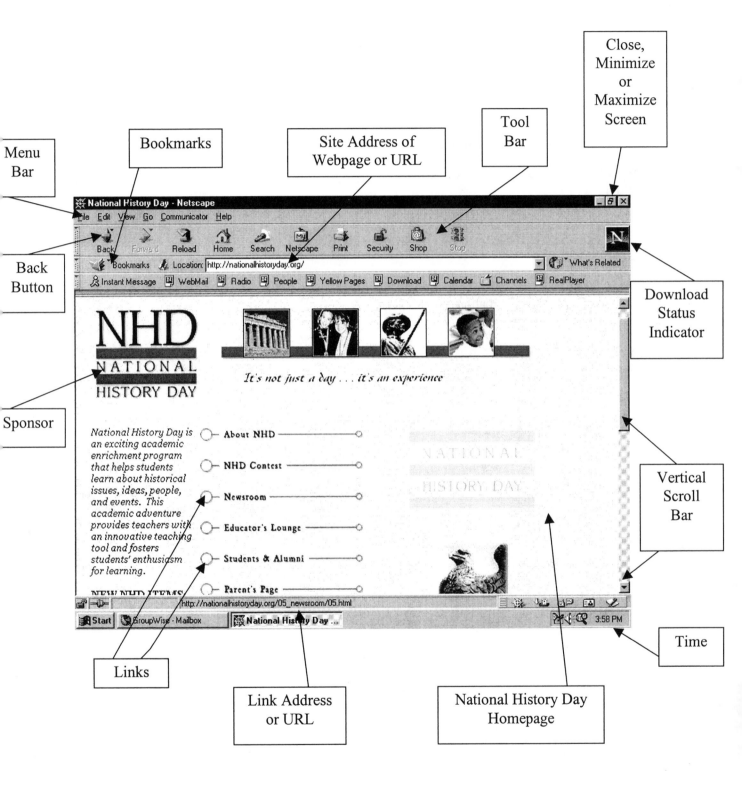

Menu Bar

Bookmarks

Site Address of Webpage or URL

Tool Bar

Close, Minimize or Maximize Screen

Back Button

Sponsor

Download Status Indicator

Vertical Scroll Bar

Time

Links

Link Address or URL

National History Day Homepage

Consider the Source

A Student Guide
To Evaluating Internet Sources
From the "CARS Checklist" developed by Robert Harris
(NHD 1999 pub.) adapted by Carlita Kosty.

Check each Internet source you use for:

I. CREDIBILITY: Can I trust this source to have correct information?
1. Check for:
   - Is the author or sponsor related to a reliable institution or government agency?
   - Are the author's credentials given?
   - Is the name of the sponsor organization given?
2. Danger clues:
   - No author or sponsor given
   - Disagrees with other information you have found
   - All negative information
   - Poor grammar, misspelled words

II. ACCURACY: Is this information factual, up to date, and complete?
1. Check for:
   - Does it give the full story? Both sides?
   - Does it show evidence of bias or prejudice?
   (If yes, it may not be useless. Different viewpoints can help the researcher understand the topic and context better.)
2. Danger clues:
   - No dates, or very old dates
   - Unclear or sweeping generalizations
   - Very one-sided view, no mention of the "other side"

III. REASONABLENESS: Is this information fair, objective, and logical?
1. Check for:
   - Does the information seem likely, possible, or probable?
   - Is it consistent? Or does it have contradictions?
   - Does it try to be fair and balanced?
2. Danger clues:
   - Outrageous or extreme language
   - Exaggerations
   - Advertising disguised as factual information

IV. SUPPORT: Does the site tell the source of facts and details used?
1. Check for:
   - Is there a bibliography?
   - Are quotes and statistics documented?
   - Can you find at least two other sources that agree with the information?
2. Danger clues:
   - No sources given for quotes, numbers, or other details
   - No other sources give similar information

Topic_____ Name_____ Date_____ Class_____

Project Progress Report
Consider the Source

Answer the following questions about the site you found most useful today.

1. What is the name or title of the website you used today?

_____

2. What is the address (URL)? _____

3. How did you locate the site?

_____ used site recommended by: _____

_____ linked from _____ site.

_____ used search engine: (which one?)_____

asked for: " _____ "

4. If you read an article, is the author given? _____
   (You will need this information for your bibliography. Be sure to write it down.)

5. Who is providing this site? (If it doesn't say, "back up" the URL until the sponsor's
   homepage appears. **If you cannot identify the author or sponsor, you better not use it!**)

_____

6. What form is the information in?

   ____image or graphic   ____statistics or graphics   ____other: _____

   ____text   ____primary source/document   _____

7. How does the information relate to your topic? _____

_____

8. How does the information you found from this source compare with what you already know
   about your topic? (agrees, disagrees, expands, contradicts, etc.)

_____

_____

9. What is the most helpful thing you found/learned on this site? _____

_____

(This is the most important question!)
10. How reliable do you think the information is? _____

    What makes you think so? _____

_____

_____

Cite the Site

I. Points to Remember

- Every source used in the project research must be listed in the bibliography, including the sources of visual material and e-mail information.

- As the World Wide Web grows and changes, the rules for citing the sources of electronic information will evolve and change, too. Be prepared to modify procedures as new forms are developed.

- It's very easy to get bogged down in complicated rules and details. Try for clarity and consistency. (Be as clear as possible and do all the Internet citations the same way.)

II. The Form for an Internet Citation

- Try to find the following information for each website used:
    1. Author or Editor (if given)
    2. Title of the Article ("put it in quotes")
    3. Title of the Complete Work (if applicable, underline)
    4. Sponsor of the website ("back up" the URL by deleting from the right end until the home page of the sponsor appears)
    5. Date of Publication (if given)
    6. URL (with no closing punctuation) inside angle brackets (<......>)
    7. Exact date you visited the website (in parentheses)

- An Internet entry in the bibliography should look like this:

"Who Invented the Cotton Gin?: A Class Debate" Whole Cloth: Discovering Science and Technology through American Textile History, Unit 2. The Lemelson Center for the Study of Invention and Innovation, National Museum of American History, Smithsonian Institution, 1998. <http://www.si.edu/lemelson/centerpieces/whole_cloth> (Sept. 14, 2000).

(no author was given for above entry)

- For e-mail use this form:
Name of Author. "Topic of correspondence." Personal e-mail (Oct. 28, 2001).

- For special cases and more information:
Ask the teacher or librarian for the *MLA Handbook for Writers of Research Papers* or check the History-Net Guide to Citing WWW Sources at
<http://h-net2.msu.edu/~africa/citation.html>

90

A Few Favorite Websites

Title	Description	URL
B.B.C.	British broadcasting news	\<http://www.bbcnc.org.uk\>
Cap Web	A guide to the U.S. Congress, links to the Senate and the House of Representatives	\<http://policy.net/capweb/congress.html\>
CNN	Current events, good maps, and graphics	\<http://www.cnn.com\>
Franklin Institute	Franklin Institute Science Museum	\<http://www.fi.edu\>
History Channel	Sponsor of National History Day	\<http://www.HistoryChannel.com\>
History Matters	Starting point for many U.S. history sources—documents, discussions, etc.	\<http://historymatters.gmu.edu\>
History Net	Many links to history magazine sources	\<http://www.TheHistoryNet.com\>
Library of Congress— American Memory Project	Catalog, exhibits, guides and links 70+ primary source collections	\<http://www.loc.gov\> \<http://memory.loc.gov/ammem/amhome.html\>
Museum Guide	Guides to museum websites	\<http://www.usc.edu/lacmnh/webmuseums\>
National Archives and Records Administration	NARA Archival Information Locator; on-line searchable database ("NAIL" is the Audiovisual Information Locator)	\<http://www.nara.gov/nara/nail.html\>
National Gallery of Art	Lots of pictures and other primary sources	\<http://www.nga.gov\>
National History Day	National History Fair—has information, ideas, and links for current year theme.	\<http://www.nationalhistoryday.org\>
National Park Service	"National Parks" includes historic places—good source for primary sources	\<http://www.nps.gov\>
Public Broadcasting System	Supplementary materials to current programming.	\<http://www.pbs.org\>
Smithsonian Institution Archives Center @ Nat'l Museum of American History	Links to museums, exhibits, collections Excellent for primary sources, especially business advertising, music, posters, other Americana	\<http://www.si.edu\> online catalog at \<www.siris.si.edu\>
U.S. Census	Census data 1950-1990	\<http://www.psc.lsa.umich.edu/SSDAN/\>
U.S. Patent Office	Original applications, diagrams, etc.	\<http://www.uspto.gov\>
White House	Good website for primary sources and information on presidents	\<http://www.whitehouse.gov\>

Glossary of Internet Terms

Back button	will take the user through all the locations and websites linked in one session, in exact reverse order.
backing up	deleting segments of the URL address, beginning at the right end, until the home page of the sponsor or parent organization appears.
bookmarks	automated way to remember specific websites.
browser	any one of the software packages that allows access to and navigation on the Web (Netscape is one example).
chat room	a text only site that allows real-time "conversations" between two or more users.
database	a site that provides a large amount of detailed information, usually organized in an easy to access format.
domain	the last part of an Internet address such as "com" or "org" indicates the site's sponsor.
download	copying a file or program from a server to a local computer.
e-mail	stands for electronic mail; individual correspondence between two computers on an Internet connection.
filter	software that allows someone to restrict access to certain areas on the Internet.
FTP	stands for File Transfer Protocol, a method of copying files from one computer to another.
hit	a match between the topic requested and websites found when using a browser.
home page	the first page a user sees when visiting a World Wide Web site.
HTML	stands for HyperText Markup Language which is used to create webpages.
HTTP	stands for HyperText Transfer Protocol, the method by which webpages are viewed on the Internet.
Internet	a global network made up of millions of computers that provide and/or receive electronic information.
IP	stands for Internet Protocol; a standard used by computers to transmit information over the Internet.
ISP	stands for Internet Service Provider; a company that provides the cable hook-up access to the Internet.

Java	(or Javascript) a computer language sometimes used in creating webpages.
link	highlighted or underlined word or picture that, when clicked, immediately links the user to another website (complete term is"hyperlink").
LAN	stands for a Local Area Network which is usually small, confined to one building or campus.
listserv	an automated mailing list that allows any member of the group to mail every other member at the same time.
netiquette	accepted proper behavior when using the Internet.
Netscape	a popular software program for searching or"browsing" the Internet.
on-line	used to describe an Internet connection (so called because telephone lines are commonly used as the connectors).
search engine	a software program that allows users to look for specific topics on the Internet without using a URL (examples are Google or Yahoo!).
server	a computer software package that allows network users to "download" or transfer files and programs to their own computers.
URL	stands for Universal Resource Locator which is the "address" used to locate websites.
WAN	stands for Wide Area Network; could be the Internet itself or a large company network.
webpage	a file containing text, pictures, and links that someone or some organization has made available on the Internet.
www	stands for World Wide Web: the entire network of websites and webpages all over the world.

VI. Campus Fair Administration

How to Use the Items in This Section

For the Campus History Fair Director

Starting a campus History Fair program can be an extremely daunting prospect. Any competition involving large numbers of students and parents must be tightly organized and carefully administered. Details matter. These suggestions, forms, and handouts will streamline the process and make it easier for everybody involved. The objective is a fun and well-run event with minimal teacher stress.

For the Parent or Student

Students should be aware of the judging criteria before the competition. Use the **Judge's Score Sheet** for the specific category (or the official National History Day judging forms in the appendix) to assess strengths and need for improvement. The folder inserts called **Information for Judges** will give students a good idea what the judges will be looking for. Use the sample interview questions to practice responding to questions. While students should not prepare speeches for the interview, and responses should be spontaneous, it never hurts to think ahead about possible answers to probable questions.

Home school students wishing to compete should contact their State History Day Coordinator. (Names and addresses are available on the NHD website. See Resources in the appendix.) While local schools may be reluctant to allow non-students into campus competition, the State History Day Coordinator can probably recommend a district or regional Fair that would be convenient and appropriate to enter. Expect to pay a registration fee.

In This Section

Organize the School Fair is a general outline of what needs to be done for a successful campus History Fair. Use it as a checklist; add special district or campus procedures as appropriate.

Set-Up, Schedules, and Awards is a detailed explanation of how to plan and run a campus competition. Time and space requirements for various categories should be consulted before selecting and reserving dates or venues.

History Fair Job Schedule is accompanied by seven folder checklists for each *job* on the schedule including the Fair Director who, presumably, makes the assignments. The Fair Director will need volunteer helpers. Typically these are history department members, but could easily include other personnel. This handout lists specific chores included in each aspect of History Fair administration. Volunteers can designate a choice or be assigned to a job or work as teams.

Finding Judges and Other Helpers gives the Fair Director some ideas for recruiting judges and suggestions for making their experience a pleasure.

(Faculty) **Request for Judges** is a handout for on-campus recruitment of judges. Enter the school name on the top line and the Fair date on the second blank line.

Judge Assignment Memo is a short form to let the volunteer judges know what they will be doing and where. Attach it to a copy of Information for Judges and distribute several days before the competition.

Expert Registry is both a letter to the school community and a form to register individuals or collections. Building a community resource database is extremely helpful and can be used by both teachers and students year after year.

Registration Instructions and **Registration Card Forms** should be used one to two weeks before the Fair. Students fill out the information requested so the detailed needs for judges, time, and space can be assessed. Remember to register projects, not students. (One card per project, regardless of the number of students in groups.)

The **Registration Card Form** can be copied onto colored cardstock and cut on a paper cutter for simple registration cards. Optionally, take the form to the district printing facility and have them made in various colors. Color-coding by category of registration cards, judges' folders, and judging forms is strongly recommended.

Information for Judges, **Examples of Judges' Comments**, and **Examples of Judges' Interview Questions** are handouts to assist novice judges through the process. Copies can be fastened inside the judges' folders containing category Score Sheets to make consultation convenient.

Judges' Score Sheets (4) are rubrics for evaluating Exhibits, Papers, Performances, or Documentaries. While National History Day recommends using the official NHD forms (found in the appendix) from the campus level on, some Fair Directors find that their judges prefer a more structured format.

The **Certificate of Participation** samples can be printed on decorated paper (available at office supply stores) for a customized History Fair award. Whether one of these forms is used or prepared certificates are purchased, each student participant should receive one.

The **Sample Announcement** may be used either as a fill-in-the-blank generic form or as an outline for a more customized listing of winners. The announcement should be made schoolwide as soon as practical after competition is complete.

Organize the School Fair

1. Get the support of essential personnel: principal, librarian, other teachers, custodian, PTA.

2. Consult the school librarian about available materials, especially primary sources. (See Primary Source Collections bibliography in the appendix.)

3. Arrange for funding: School? District? PTA? Grant? Community? Businesses?

4. Select date, site, and time: Put it on the official school calendar as early as possible.

5. Meet with department teachers to divide up jobs.

6. Make an announcement: Memo to faculty? School newsletter? Student newspaper? Posters?

7. Recruit judges: Start with the school faculty and administrators, if possible.

8. Register projects: Color code everything.

9. THE CAMPUS HISTORY FAIR.

10. Debrief immediately. Save the notes for next year.

11. Thank everyone.

12. Meet with winners and parents to prepare for the next level of competition.

Set-Up, Schedules, and Awards
for the Campus History Fair

Careful planning is necessary for a smooth running Campus History Fair. This is an exciting, tense, and busy moment for student contestants and their parents. The details of assigning space and times for project presentation, structuring competition fairly, and arranging the awards for winners really do matter.

1. **Space for Exhibits**
   - History Fair exhibits are usually set-up in a library, cafeteria, or gym.
   - Each exhibit must have a table top area of 40" wide X 30" deep. Some exhibits may be free-standing and therefore require floor space.
   - A week or two before students actually register, teachers can probably estimate the number of exhibit projects their students will enter, so arrangements can be made ahead of time for adequate exhibit space and judges.
   - Tables can be set in rows or in pods, exhibits facing all one way or back to back, depending on the size of the table and the shape of the facility where the judging will take place.
   - If an Open House for parents is planned after judging, keep in mind the space needed for viewer traffic and for photographs.
   - Some exhibits may need electrical outlets. Teachers and/or registration cards should give this information and it should be noted when the project is assigned a number and location. Warn students about leaving valuable artifacts or equipment out during Open House.
   - Assign one team of judges to every ten to twelve exhibits. A large number of entries may require a second round of judging to determine the winner.

2. **Rooms and Times for Performances and Documentaries**
   - The rules for both categories give students ten minutes to present, five minutes to set up and five minutes to take down (sets, equipment, etc.) and judges need to interview the student(s) for about five minutes. Average time per project is around twenty minutes, or three per hour.
   - Judges should not be asked to work more than two hours, or evaluate more than six projects, especially if the judges are teachers and the judging is after school. If necessary, schedule judging sessions over several days and hold the "finals" on the day of the Campus Fair.
   - Performances need to be scheduled in a fairly soundproof room or an isolated area. Ambient noise and commotion needs to be minimum so presentations can be easily heard by the judges and neither the judges nor the contestants will be distracted.
   - Documentaries need a location with access to audiovisual technology, computers, and a projection system.
   - Both documentaries and performances should have a "waiting area" for students and their sets and costumes or equipment. A teacher or a parent volunteer should supervise and help keep them on schedule.
   - Both categories are the type of thing teachers, parents, and other students want to see. Decide ahead of time what the policy will be about allowing visitors during judging. Whatever the choice, all should be absolutely silent and take care to enter and leave a judging room only between presentations.

3. Competition

- Decide to compete within grade levels or by category. Competition within grade levels allows younger students equal opportunity to win and/or advance. Category competition is the standard for all advanced competitions such as State History Day and National History Day. One popular and practical model has the Exhibits category competition by grade level and all other entries by their category, regardless of grade. This arrangement allows for the popularity of the Exhibits category, which usually draws more participation than all the other categories combined.
- Every project deserves to be judged by someone other than the student's teacher. With a large number of entries, especially in the Exhibits category, consider having "room fairs" preliminary to the Campus Fair, or have History Fair teachers trade projects and judge each others' entries as a "first round" of judging, giving the top entries to the "official" judges to determine the Campus Fair winners.
- Decide on a system for assigning project numbers so they will be easily recognizable to both teachers and volunteers. Prefixes could indicate grade level, category, or teacher. Group project numbers should be different from those for individual projects.
- Once the structure of the competition is decided, estimate the number of projects in each division and the number of judges needed. Papers and exhibits should be limited to ten entries per judging team of two or three, while performances and documentaries require one team of judges for every five to six entries.
- For Papers category, set a deadline one or two days before the Campus Fair. Judges who volunteer to judge Papers can take them home to read. Make enough copies for each judge to have one, place in a folder with guidelines and judging forms. Keep one copy of each Paper for the Fair Director and one for the teacher. Once again, the limit per judge is ten to twelve. Judges can then meet the day of the Campus Fair and compare choices to select the winners.
- Arrange for a "judges' room" where judges can confer and fill in their forms. If convenient, the person responsible for placing ribbons and making announcements should be there, as well as the Fair Director to answer questions and keep everyone on schedule. Having refreshments available will help the process along.
- Encourage judges to write positive comments and describe things to improve and give specific suggestions. Students really take judges' comments very seriously—so remember students have feelings and parents.

4. Awards

- Arrange for First, Second, Third, and Honorable Mention in each of the seven categories, plus any Special Awards you intend to give. (Special Awards could include African American History, Women's History, Colonial and Revolutionary History, Oral History, Hispanic History, etc.)
- Order ribbons or prizes well ahead of the competition. Request the maximum number of ribbons/prizes that may be needed, counting a possible five students in each group category and the Special Awards. Save leftovers for next year.
- It's nice for the students, and good public relations, to have prize ribbons placed on the Exhibits and Papers for Open House. Also, announce winners of Performances and Documentaries, or list them prominently on a board or poster.
- Consider having a People's Choice award for Exhibits if the student body will view the entries, or have visitors vote at the Open House.
- Announce winners as soon as possible and in as many places as possible. Certainly, a school announcement should be made, but also consider newsletters, school websites, or local media.
- Every participant should receive a certificate as soon as possible after the Campus Fair is completed.

- Winners and their parents should be contacted immediately, either by the teacher or the Fair Director, to discuss advancing to the next level of competition. Items to consider are dates and deadlines, registration, and project revision.
- All student contestants should receive a Certificate of Participation and all winners should receive ribbons, including each member of groups. These can be distributed at a formal ceremony or teachers can distribute in class.
- It's nice to have something students can wear. Middle schoolers especially like to be recognized. Consider buttons when they enter a project or a special field trip for the winners.

5. Thank Everyone
- The Fair Director and other chairpersons should keep a list of people who helped make the Fair a success other than the judges. These might include the librarian, the computer teacher, the drama teacher, the custodian, or the PTA, and so on. The Fair Director should thank them directly with a written note and the Publicity Chairperson should make sure they are mentioned in announcements.
- The Judges Chairperson should keep a list of the judges, both staff and off-campus. All judges should receive an individual thank-you note, even if it is computer generated. A small thank-you gift is also appropriate.

History Fair
Job Schedule

1. DIRECTOR_____
___ Coordinate all activities/Advise and assist as needed.
___ Provide Rules information, student handouts, and supplies.
___ Train judges, provide handouts, assist Judges Chairman with assignments, and other duties.
___ Provide list for invitations off-campus (Central Office and other schools).
___ Coordinate with Central Office and other District schools for District Fair, if needed.
___ Organize, supervise, and chaperone participants who advance to Regional competition.

2. PUBLICITY_____
___ Arrange for student-made posters.
___ Design and print invitations. Give some to Hospitality and distribute others to teachers.
___ Arrange for all announcements, including information on winners (photos if possible) to District Publicity Coordinator.
___ Contact local newspaper education editor and/or local television station.

3. REGISTRATION_____
___ Arrange for printed, color-coded registration cards.
___ Write instruction handout for teachers; copy and make demo transparencies; distribute to teachers.
___ Collect registration cards from teachers: organize, check information, spelling, special awards qualification, or requests for electrical outlets, floor space, etc.
___ Number, tally, and give to Set-Up.

4. JUDGES_____
___ Recruit judges from faculty and staff. Assist Director with assignment and training of judges.
___ Make folders for judges with information handouts, sample remarks and questions, color-coded score sheets with project numbers and titles entered. Provide judges with ribbons/name-tags and sharpened pencils.
___ Tally score sheets as received during judging. Make lists of winners for Director, Publicity, and Awards. Sort by teacher for easy return.
___ Write thank-you notes to judges after Fair.
NOTE: For a large campus fair the Judges Chairman will need an assistant, or two.

5. SET-UP AND CHECK-IN _____
___ Using Registration cards, organize Fair location giving each project a place and/or time.
___ Set up display area with project numbers if possible.
___ Make a map or diagram of Exhibits area and Performance/Documentary rooms for contestants and Open House visitors—copies and/or posters.
___ Supervise (or arrange for supervision of) Check-In of Exhibits on Fair day, and removal from display area after Open House or after viewing by students and parents.

6. HOSPITALITY_____
___ Address and mail off-campus invitations.
___ Arrange for all refreshments: Judges' training session, during judging, and the History Fair Open House.
___ Be available to greet visitors during judging and Open House, serve refreshments.
___ Arrange for food area clean-up and leftovers after the Fair.

7. AWARDS_____
___ Order and pick up ribbons and certificates.
___ Assist Judges to place ribbons on winning Exhibits before Open House.
___ Fill out and distribute student ribbons and participation certificates to teachers.
___ Count and label left-over ribbons, certificates, and other supplies, before packing away for next year.

*ALL: Keep a list of people to thank for their help with the Fair.

Campus History Fair Director

___ Coordinate all activities/Advise and assist as needed.

___ Provide Rules information, student handouts, and supplies.

___ Train judges, provide handouts assist Judges Chairman with assignments, and other duties.

___ Provide list for invitations off-campus (Central Office and other schools).

___ Coordinate with Central Office and other District schools for District Fair, if needed.

___ Organize, supervise, and chaperone students who advance to Regional competition.

___ Other: _____

__ _____

__ _____

__ _____

__ _____

__ _____

__ _____

__ _____

People to Thank:

_____ **For:** _____

_____ _____

_____ _____

_____ _____

_____ _____

History Fair
Publicity

___ Arrange for student-made posters.

___ Design and print invitations. Give some to Hospitality and distribute others to teachers.

___ Compose and submit all announcements, including information on winners (photos if possible) to District Publicity Coordinator.

___ Contact local newspaper education editor and/or local television station.

___ Other: _____

__ _____

__ _____

__ _____

__ _____

__ _____

__ _____

__ _____

People to Thank:

_____ **For:** _____

_____ _____

_____ _____

_____ _____

_____ _____

History Fair
Registration

___ Arrange for printed, color-coded registration cards.

___ Write instruction handout for teachers; copy and make demo transparencies; distribute to teachers.

___ Collect registration cards from teachers: organize, check information, spelling, and special awards.

___ Number, tally, and give to Set-Up.

___ Other: _____

___ _____

___ _____

___ _____

___ _____

___ _____

___ _____

___ _____

People to Thank:

_____ **For:** _____

_____   _____

_____   _____

_____   _____

_____   _____

History Fair
Judges

___ Recruit judges from faculty, staff, and community.

___ Contact off-campus judges from last year to request their time again this year.

___ Assist Director with assignment and training of judges—print handouts, be available during judging.

___ Make folders and copy handouts for judges. Print score sheets. Enter project numbers and titles.

Color code: _____ exhibits are   _____

_____ exhibits are   _____

_____ exhibits are   _____

Performances are   _____

Documentaries are   _____

Papers are _____

___ Provide judges with ribbons/name-tags and sharpened pencils.

___ Tally judges' score sheets as received during judging. Make lists of winners for Director, Publicity, and Awards. Sort by teacher after tally, then return to teachers ASAP. (Students will be clamoring for them!)

___ Write thank-you notes to judges after Fair.

___ Other: _____

___ _____

___ _____

___ _____

People to Thank:

_____ **For:** _____

_____   _____

_____   _____

History Fair
Set-Up and Check-In

___ Using Registration cards, organize Fair location giving each project a place and/or time.

___ Set up display area with project numbers if possible.

___ Make a map or diagram of Exhibits area and Performance/Documentary rooms for contestants and Open House visitors—copies and/or posters.

___ Supervise (or arrange for supervision of) Check-In of Exhibits on Fair day, and removal from display area after Open House or after viewing by students and parents.

___ Other: _____

___ _____

___ _____

___ _____

___ _____

___ _____

___ _____

___ _____

___ _____

People to Thank:

_____ **For:** _____

_____   _____

_____   _____

_____   _____

_____   _____

History Fair
Hospitality

___ Address and mail off-campus invitations.

___ Arrange for all refreshments: For Judges' training session(s), Judging after school and for History Fair Open House.

Times: _____

_____

___ Be available to greet visitors during judging and Open House, serve refreshments.

___ Arrange for food area clean-up and leftovers after the Fair.

___ Other: _____

__ _____

__ _____

__ _____

__ _____

__ _____

__ _____

__ _____

People to Thank:

_____ **For:** _____

_____ _____

_____ _____

_____ _____

_____ _____

History Fair
Awards

____ Order and pick up ribbons and certificates.

____ Assist Judges to place ribbons on winning Exhibits before Open House.

____ Fill out and distribute student prize ribbons and participation certificates to teachers to give to students in their classes.

____ Count and label left-over ribbons, certificates, buttons, and other supplies before packing away for next year.

____ Other: _____

____ _____

____ _____

____ _____

____ _____

____ _____

____ _____

____ _____

People to Thank:

_____ **For:** _____

_____ _____

_____ _____

_____ _____

_____ _____

Finding Judges and Other Helpers

- Start with the school **faculty**, administrators, PTA, secretaries and aides: Judges don't have to be historians to judge History Fair projects if they receive appropriate training and guidelines. Also consider asking a drama coach, an A/V/media person, a computer teacher, and the librarian to assist students with project preparation.

- Local **historical societies** and **museums** usually have lists of able volunteers.

- Check with history **teachers from other schools** in the district or in the county.

- History professors from area **colleges and universities** are usually more than willing to help out. Contact the history department of the institution and explain what is needed. Many will be familiar with the program already.

- For **Special Award** categories: Contact area ethnic, civic, or religious organizations associated with the award (e.g., NAACP for Black History Award; LULAC for Hispanic History Award; DAR for Revolutionary War Award)

SOME SUGGESTIONS

- Each project should be judged by two or three judges; no judge should have to evaluate more than ten to twelve projects, fewer for Performances and Documentaries. For a large school fair, the history teachers can hold preliminary class fairs or schedule two rounds of judging on Fair day.

- Plan the judging event after school or in the evening for the convenience of the judges. For a school fair, two hours should be sufficient. If possible, plan an Open House for parents and community to view the Exhibits after judging.

- Feed them! Feed the judges when you train them (AM doughnuts and coffee, PM chips, dips and sodas) and feed them while they are judging—something substantial if they will be working two hours after school.

- Always send out reminders a couple of days before, and thank-you notes immediately after.

- Well-prepared judges are essential for the fair to run smoothly. Take time to make a copy of project guidelines for each volunteer to study before the event and have extra copies available during judging (also for parents who want to know the judging criteria).

- Make sure judges understand that they are not grading the projects, only ranking them. Teachers do the grading for class.

- Name-tags, ribbons, or badges for all judges, school staff as well as visitors.

- The decision of the judges is final. **This is not negotiable.**

Annual History Fair
on

_____

WE NEED JUDGES!!   PLEASE VOLUNTEER.

*No experience necessary.
*All staff members welcome.
* Refreshments served.
* On-the-job training.

- What grade(s) do you teach or work with? _____

Sign here to volunteer:

(Please mark 2 choices)

- **Historical Papers**   We need _____ judges:
  Date(s) _____   Time_____

  _____

- _____ grade **Exhibits**   We need _____ judges:
  Date(s) _____   Time _____

  _____

- _____ grade **Exhibits**   We need _____ judges:
  Date(s) _____   Time _____

  _____

- _____ grade **Exhibits**   We need _____ judges:
  Date(s) _____   Time _____

  _____

- **Performances**   We need _____ judges:
  Date(s)_____

  _____

- **Documentaries**   We need _____ judges:
  Date(s) _____

  _____

- **Special Awards** (African American History, Women's History, Colonial and Revolutionary History, etc.) May also be asked to serve as "tie breakers."

  We need _____ judges:

  _____

PLEASE RETURN TO _____

THANKS!!

History Fair
Judge's Assignment

Dear _____,

Thank you for volunteering to judge the _____ History Fair

   on _____.

- Your assignment is: _____.

- Please report to _____ at _____.

- There will be a short training session, then judging will begin at _____.

- Attached is a copy of the judging criteria for your information.

Thanks again for your help!

History Fair
Judge's Assignment

Dear _____,

Thank you for volunteering to judge the _____ History Fair

   on _____.

- Your assignment is: _____.

- Please report to _____ at _____.

- There will be a short training session, then judging will begin at _____.

- Attached is a copy of the judging criteria for your information.

Thanks again for your help!

Expert Registry

Dear Parent, Colleague, or Community Member,

This year the _____ School History Department will be participating in History Fair. This is a national program that begins at the campus level and concludes each year with National History Day in June at the University of Maryland. We hope this will be a really great experience for our students.

In a few weeks students will begin researching various historical topics to prepare for the campus History Fair on _____. All topics must fit an annual theme. This year's theme is "_____." Students are encouraged to use primary source materials and interviews in their research, in addition to standard modes of research such as libraries and the Internet. In order to assist students in this pursuit, we are attempting to build a database of local "experts" on various topics.

Do you have a collection of old pictures? Are you widely read on a particular time period, person, or event? Have you ever lived in a foreign country? Are you a veteran of a war? Did you participate in the Civil Rights Movement or the Peace Movement? Do you have an interesting or unusual hobby or skill? Almost everyone has expertise in something, so think what yours is then fill out and send in the **Expert Registry** form below. You may just have or know exactly what a student is looking for. We really appreciate your willingness to help. Please understand that if you aren't called this year, your name will remain in our database and you may be contacted next year. You may return the completed form to _____. If you have any questions, please contact _____ at_____.

Thanks,

_____
History Fair Director

****

History Fair
Expert Registry

Name_____   Phone: home _____

Best place/time to reach me: office _____

_____   e-mail _____

Please tell us the topic or topics on which you have knowledge and would be willing to have a student interview you; or collections, experience, or skills you would be willing to share with a student.

SUBJECT   DESCRIPTION / DETAILS

_____   _____

                                      _____

_____   _____

                                      _____

History Fair
Registration Instructions

1. Register projects, not students. **One card per project.**

2. Students should MAKE SURE they write clearly and spell correctly. If they win, these cards will be used to write announcements and to register them for Regional Competition—probably by someone who doesn't know them. So . . . **print clearly**.

3. **COLOR CODE:** _____ = _____ grade exhibits
   _____ = _____ grade exhibits
   _____ = _____ grade exhibits
   _____ = Performances—all grades
   _____ = Documentaries—all grades
   _____ = Papers—all grades

3. Leave #_____ BLANK. This will be filled in later when the project is assigned a place or a time and an entry number.

4. Special Award categories are:
   - **African American History**
   - **Women's History**
   - **Oral History**
   - **Hispanic History**
   - **Colonial/Revolutionary America**

5. Teachers should keep a list of their entries—or copy the cards before turning them in to the Registrar(s).

6. Teachers should grade projects either before Fair judging, or after. Do not allow the judges to do this. They will only rank projects within the group they are assigned. (Teachers may give bonus points to winners.)

7. Exhibits and Papers should have NO NAMES anywhere. Paperwork carries only title, category, and project number. Performances and Documentaries cannot be anonymous as students must be present at the time of judging, but paperwork still should have only title, category, and project number on the title page.

8. If your exhibit or performance will need an electrical outlet, please note this under "Special Requests" on the registration card.

History Fair Project # _____

Title: _____
Topic: _____ Teacher: _____
Students—PLEASE PRINT CLEARLY and CORRECTLY
1. _____ 4. _____
2. _____ 5. _____
3. _____

CATEGORY (circle one)

Paper Individual Exhibit Group Exhibit Individual Documentary
Group Documentary Individual Performance Group Performance

Special Award Category? _____
Special equipment or location? _____
Other special request? _____

History Fair Project # _____

Title: _____
Topic: _____ Teacher: _____
Students—PLEASE PRINT CLEARLY and CORRECTLY
1. _____ 4. _____
2. _____ 5. _____
3. _____

CATEGORY (circle one)

Paper Individual Exhibit Group Exhibit Individual Documentary
Group Documentary Individual Performance Group Performance

Special Award Category? _____
Special equipment or location? _____
Other special request? _____

History Fair Project # _____

Title: _____
Topic: _____ Teacher: _____
Students—PLEASE PRINT CLEARLY and CORRECTLY
1. _____ 4. _____
2. _____ 5. _____
3. _____

CATEGORY (circle one)

Paper Individual Exhibit Group Exhibit Individual Documentary
Group Documentary Individual Performance Group Performance

Special Award Category? _____
Special equipment or location? _____
Other special request? _____

History Fair Project # _____

Title: _____
Topic: _____ Teacher: _____
Students—PLEASE PRINT CLEARLY and CORRECTLY
1. _____ 4. _____
2. _____ 5. _____
3. _____

CATEGORY (circle one)

Paper Individual Exhibit Group Exhibit Individual Documentary
Group Documentary Individual Performance Group Performance

Special Award Category? _____
Special equipment or location? _____
Other special request? _____

Information for Judges

- Judges do NOT grade projects. Teachers do. Judges choose the best from their assigned group of projects and rank them based on the score sheet criteria. Please select 1st, 2nd, 3rd, and Honorable Mention.

- Exhibits and Papers Judges may work as a team or individually—Judges' choice, but consensus is necessary. Documentary and Performance judges need to work as teams since students only present once.

- Please DO write comments on the judging forms ESPECIALLY on those that you feel have potential for the next level of competition.

- All projects should fit the theme: "_____"
This should be clear in the presentation and the project narrative.

- Projects—papers, displays, performances, documentaries—should tell the entire story. Judges should not need "background" to understand the topic. Nor should supplementary materials be necessary. Documentaries should not have (or need) live narration.

- **Process Narrative**—All projects except Papers have a one- to two-page paper (maximum 500 words) telling how the topic fits the theme, why the topic was chosen, and how the project was developed. This is NOT the "story." (The "story" should be complete in the exhibit, documentary, or performance—see above.)

- **Annotated Bibliography**—All projects. Primary sources should be listed first and may be given more weight. Standard and consistent form should be used. Annotations may be brief descriptions of the source and/or how it was used.

- All projects should adhere to size/length limitations: Exhibits, 30" x 40" x 72"; Papers, 2500 words (1500 minimum); Documentaries and Performances, 10 minutes.

Things to Look For:

- Based on good, solid history with evidence of research.

- Shows insight, significance, and analysis; not just a report.

- Shows the story in context of other events and the bigger picture.

- Uses Primary Sources
"Firsthand" information sources from the time of the topic events such as journals, interviews with witnesses or participants, contemporary accounts, ads, songs, photographs, artifacts, recordings, etc.

- Has potential for advanced competition.
Winners use judges' comments to revise and improve projects before going on.

THANKS FOR YOUR TIME!

Examples of Judges' Comments

Positive/Strengths

- Original/challenging topic choice.

- Very well organized.

- Attractive/logical layout.

- Good primary sources.

- Excellent use of the theme.

- Very attractive (or entertaining).

- Thanks for teaching me a history lesson.

- Good use of available sources.

- Attractive use of color/graphics/layout.

- Excellent ideas/analysis.

- Interesting interpretation of facts.

- Process narrative is very well written.

Areas Needing Improvement

- Perhaps captions (or paper) should have been proofread more carefully.

- A little more research would really improve this project.

- Primary sources would add authenticity to your research.

- Need to emphasize the theme more.

- A little more practice (or work) would have made this an excellent project.

- All sources need to be annotated (or cited).

- Need to check on bibliography form.

- Please watch the size/time rules—you don't want to be disqualified on a technicality.

The Interview
Examples of Judges' Questions

- What was your most useful source? Why? How did you use it?

- What would you have done if you were . . . ?

- What do you think was the most important achievement/result of . . . ?

- What do we have today that came from this? Or that is like this?

- What did you learn personally from this project?

- What got you interested in this topic?

- Why did you choose this category?

- Is there anything we haven't asked that you would like to tell us about your project?

Historical Paper
Judge's Score Sheet

Title _____ Judge _____

	0 None	1 Minimal	2 Satisfactory	3 Good	4 Excellent
I. HISTORICAL PRESENTATION 60% Shows solid research? Facts are accurate? Context, Analysis, and Interpretation? Tells the whole story? Change over time? Effective use of sources? Including primary sources? COMMENTS:					
II. THEME 20% How well does the project relate to the theme " _____ _____ " (paper should demonstrate this clearly) COMMENTS:					

III. RULES   10%
  A. **Length**: 1500 to 2500 words
  B. **Citations**: either footnotes or endnotes
     Standard, consistent form
  C. **Type**: plain font, no oversize print
  D. **Annotated Bibliography**:
     At least five sources?
     Adequate annotations?
     Primary sources? Separated and listed first?
     Proper and consistent bibliography form?
COMMENTS:					

IV. APPEARANCE 10% Has focus? Makes sense? Attractive and easy to read? Correct spelling and grammar? Gives detail and/or examples? COMMENTS:					

OVERALL COMMENTS:_____

THANKS!

Entry # _____   Place _____

Exhibit
Judge's Score Sheet

Title _____   Judge _____

	0 None	1 Minimal	2 Satisfactory	3 Good	4 Excellent
I. HISTORICAL PRESENTATION 60% Shows solid research? Facts are accurate? Context, Analysis, and Interpretation? Tells the whole story? Change over time? Effective use of sources? Including primary sources? COMMENTS:					
II. THEME 10% How well does the project relate to the theme? "_____ _____" (project should demonstrate this clearly) COMMENTS:					

III. PAPERWORK 20%
  A. **Process Narrative**:
    Does it tell how the topic fits the theme?
    How the project was researched and developed?
    Significance and impact of the topic in history?
  B. **Annotated Bibliography**:
    At least five sources?
    Adequate annotations?
    Primary sources? Separated and listed first?
    Proper and consistent bibliography form?
COMMENTS:					

IV. APPEARANCE 10% Has focus? Makes sense? Clear and logical layout or format? Neat and attractive? Creative design, color? Captions appropriate? Use of documents? COMMENTS:					
OVERALL COMMENTS: _____					

THANKS!

Performance
Judge's Score Sheet

Title _____ Judge _____

	0 None	**1** Minimal	**2** Satisfactory	**3** Good	**4** Excellent
I. HISTORICAL PRESENTATION 60% Shows solid research? Facts are accurate? Context, Analysis, and Interpretation? Tells the whole story? Change over time? Effective use of sources? Including primary sources? COMMENTS:					
II. THEME 10% How well does the project relate to the theme? "_____ _____" (project should demonstrate this clearly) COMMENTS:					

III. PAPERWORK 20%
  A. **Process Narrative:**
    Does it tell how the topic fits the theme?
    How the project was researched and developed?
    Significance and impact of the topic in history?
  B. **Annotated Bibliography:**
    At least five sources?
    Adequate annotations?
    Primary sources? Separated and listed first?
    Proper and consistent bibliography form?
COMMENTS:					

IV. PRESENTATION 10% Introduction/setting? Story flows/makes sense? Uses time effectively? (10 min. limit) Stage presence and voice clarity? Appropriate props/costumes? Paced/blocked? Overall impact? COMMENTS:					

OVERALL COMMENTS: _____

THANKS!

Documentary
Judge's Score Sheet

Title _____ Judge _____

	0 None	**1** Minimal	**2** Satisfactory	**3** Good	**4** Excellent
I. HISTORICAL PRESENTATION 60% Shows solid research? Facts are accurate? Context, Analysis, and Interpretation? Tells the whole story? Change over time? Effective use of sources? Including primary sources? COMMENTS:					
II. THEME 10% How well does the project relate to the theme? " _____ _____ " (project should demonstrate this clearly) COMMENTS:					

III. PAPERWORK 20%
  A. **Process Narrative**:
    Does it tell how the topic fits the theme?
    How the project was researched and developed?
    Significance and impact of the topic in history?
  B. **Annotated Bibliography**:
    At least five sources?
    Adequate annotations?
    Primary sources? Separated and listed first?
    Proper and consistent bibliography form?
COMMENTS:					

IV. USE OF TECHNOLOGY 10% Does presentation show importance of topic? Does it tell the whole "story"? Is it original and creative? Appropriate use of illustrations, voice? music? Images clear? Primary sources/interviews? Efficient use of time? (10 min. limit) COMMENTS:					
OVERALL COMMENTS: _____					

THANKS!

Certificate of Participation

in the

_____

History Fair

is awarded to

_____

Presented by _____

at _____

this _____ day of _____, _____

Certificate of Achievement

is awarded to

_____

for

Participation in the _____ History Fair.

Presented by _____ at

this _____ day of _____ , _____

Announcing the Winners

Please announce on: _____

HISTORY FAIR NEWS

Yesterday the _____ History Department held the
_____ Annual School History Fair. _____ projects were entered by _____ students.
The quality of the projects was outstanding. Winning display projects will be on exhibit in
_____ through _____.

Here are the winners:

HISTORICAL PAPERS CATEGORY
    1st _____
    2nd _____
    3rd _____
    HM_____

EXHIBIT CATEGORY:
Individual
    1st _____
    2nd_____
    3rd _____
    HM_____
Groups
    1st _____
    _____
    2nd_____
    _____
    3rd_____
    _____
    HM_____
    _____

SPECIAL AWARDS:
    • _____ to: _____
    • _____ to: _____
    • _____ to: _____
    • _____ to: _____
    • _____ to: _____

PERFORMANCE CATEGORY
Individual
1st _____
2nd_____
3rd_____
HM_____
Groups
1st _____
_____
2nd_____
_____
3rd_____
_____
HM_____
_____

DOCUMENTARY CATEGORY
Individual
1st _____
2nd_____
3rd_____
HM_____
Groups
1st _____
_____
2nd_____
_____
3rd_____
_____
HM_____
_____

All these students are to be congratulated for their fine work. _____ will be contacting those eligible to advance to District/Regional competition. All students who entered the Fair should be very proud of their accomplishments. This was a major undertaking and required extraordinary effort and dedication.

_____ wishes to thank all the teachers who so generously assisted by serving as judges and by helping both students and teachers in a multitude of ways to prepare projects for competition. **Special thanks goes to**:

_____
_____
_____

VII. Advanced Competition

How to Use the Items in This Section

For Teacher, History Fair Coach, or Parent

Success at advanced levels of competition requires hard work and careful planning. Bearing in mind that students may revise and enhance their projects at each stage, the suggestions and hand-outs in this section will help develop winning projects. They can be used by students, teachers, and parents. The ultimate goal is a trip to Washington, D.C., and a chance to participate in National History Day, a four-day competition event held each June at the University of Maryland in College Park.

Parents are extremely important at this stage because they will be called upon not only for advice and permission, but also for transportation and financial support. Very few contestants are able to compete successfully without the complete support of their parents.

In This Section

What If They Win? is a list of practical questions the teacher, the History Fair Director, and the parent should consider as soon as the project qualifies for advanced competition.

Fundraising presents a plan and some possible sources of money to cover the expenses of advanced competition. Ideally, the students should not have to worry about this. Unfortunately, the reality is that some schools either cannot afford, or do not support, students to out-of-town or out-of-state competitions.

Coaching Winners offers some suggestions for the teacher or parent who assumes responsibility for preparing the students for the next event. At this point what may have started as a class project becomes a major extracurricular activity. All students need guidance as they expand their research, act on judges' suggestions, and improve their presentations.

What the Judges Expect explains in detail the high standards and expectations at State or National History Day competitions.

Some Advice from a Winner gives specific suggestions from a veteran contestant and National History Day finalist.

The **Regional History Fair Participants** information handout lets students know the details and deadlines of advanced competition and describes their responsibilities. Although this example is for a Regional History Fair, similar announcements should be used for District, State, or other off-campus contests.

The **Regional Information Letter to Parents** is an example of keeping everyone informed. This same format can be used for District or State competitions. The teacher-coach needs to keep in close contact with parents and resolve any problems as soon as they surface.

Out-of-Town Competition Travel Permission/Parent Release form is strongly recommended for any History Fair trips where the parents are not accompanying students. Check to see if the school or school district already has such a form and wants their own used. Chaperoning students can be full of legal pitfalls if all the proper forms are not signed and in place before leaving. While checking on permission forms, teachers might ask about reimbursement for travel expenses, too.

The **Thank You Letter to Parents**, or some version thereof, can be used to let the parents know how much their support is appreciated. Don't pass up the opportunity to impress on them the value of the History Fair program in their child's education.

What If They Win?
Some Practical Matters to Consider

- Hold an organizational meeting with students and their parents to determine if everyone is committed and available for the next competition event. Make sure both parents and students understand what is involved. Then check calendars—personal, family, and school. Mark or reserve dates as needed.

- Check school or district policy on sponsoring students to advanced competition. Does sponsorship include financial support? If so, what does it cover? (If not, see the Fundraising handout in this section.) What permission or release forms are required? What type of insurance is available?

- In group projects one student will become the group leader and contact person. Decide who will serve in this capacity with great care and after consultation with the parents.

- Register on time. Make sure all parts, and all participants, are included.

- Make reservations for lodging as well as transportation, as appropriate. If possible, consult with a previous year's contestant or sponsor about what to expect.

- Investigate options and costs for transporting exhibit boards, sets and props, or A/V equipment. Be sure to include these expenses when a budget is developed either for the sponsoring school district or to present in fundraising proposals.

- Make a list of improvements to be made, people to interview, museums or other sites to visit. Block in calendars and divide up chores.

- Decide who is going to supervise the project during revision: the classroom teacher, the History Fair Director, or the parent.

- Make sure everybody has a copy of the official National History Day *Rule Book* (see Resources in the appendix). This is the final word on rules.

- Most copyrighted material may be used by students in their projects without specific permission as long as appropriate credit is given. However, if there is any doubt, now is the time to contact the publisher or copyright holder and ask for written permission. This works easily if the teacher makes the request on school letterhead.

- Be advised that at National History Day and at many state competitions, firearms of any kind, even toys or models, are strictly prohibited. This rule applies to Exhibits and Performances.

- When it's over, thank everyone. The students themselves should write notes to all those people who assisted either with the project or with financial support. Teachers should thank administrators, colleagues, or others who assisted, and even parents. Personal touches like snapshots of the students with their projects or copies of newspaper articles are appropriate items to enclose with the notes of thanks.

Fundraising

Some **ideas** on raising money to sponsor students to Advanced Competition - State or National History Day:

- Before asking for financial support from individuals, associations, companies, or requesting approval for a school fundraising project, work out a detailed budget of expenses and funding already available. Be as specific as possible about needs and available resources.

- If possible work through a school district or community nonprofit foundation so all donations can be tax-deductible for the donors whether they are corporations or individuals.

- Don't be shy about asking for money. The student is representing the school, the school district, and the community when participating in advanced competition.

Some possible funding **sources** to consider:

- Start with typical school fundraisers like bake sales or car washes.

- Sell buttons or T-shirts: "Send Judy to Nationals" or "I Helped Send the Eisenhower Project to Washington. Middlebury High School, 2002"

- Check local civic organizations and women's clubs. Also church or religious groups and auxiliaries.

- Special interest groups associated with the topic.

- Don't forget the teachers, and their friends, as well as professional education associations.

- International, cultural, or ethnic associations, especially those associated with the topic.

- Chambers of Commerce can refer educators to local merchants who actively support educational programs. Also check franchise sports teams.

- Local historical associations, museums, or living history groups may have grant money available for competition expenses.

- Some cities have scholarship or youth advancement funds available. Check with the mayor's office or the city council.

Coaching Winners

The teacher who is fortunate enough to have students advance to Regional, State or National History Day already has winners. Here are some ideas on improving projects and increasing the students' appreciation, understanding and confidence before the next contest.

- Don't pick favorites during the classroom phase of project development. Allow the students to sort themselves out during campus and/or school district competitions. Then focus time and energy on the winners.

- Set up a schedule of regular meetings with the students to check progress, offer suggestions, answer questions, and make plans. Once a week is ideal. Include parents as appropriate.

- Brainstorm with the students for possible sources to enhance research. "Who would know . . . ?" "Where would they have . . . ?" Make lists, plan field trips, make contacts for interviews, and ask about borrowing artifacts or documents.

- The teacher-coach should be well-informed on the project topic and will probably become somewhat of an expert before all is over and done, especially if the project advances to National competition.

- Cultivate contacts among local academics, community leaders, museum curators, historical society members, etc., who can help students find people to interview on specific topics.

- Ask a librarian to double-check all primary source references. Make sure the students can explain why and how each is primary to the topic.

- Practice interview questions. Invite colleagues to join in or contribute practice questions.

- Be sure to try out all equipment, sets, props, costumes, layouts, and the like, before the event. Time (measure, or count words) exactly. Frequently the projects in finals at advanced competitions are all excellent. When faced with difficult choices, judges may have to eliminate projects with rule infractions.

- Classroom teachers and parents should bear in mind that preparing a competitive entry requires a lot of time. History teachers can adjust class assignments accordingly and parents may consider limiting household or family responsibilities for the duration.

What the Judges Expect

- Focus on a topic that impacts people's lives.

- Make sure you can prove everything you say.

- Be creative in the search for primary sources. Look at autobiographies for quotes. Check useful secondary source bibliographies for primary sources the author used. Songs and ads contemporary to the topic can portray popular opinion or social climate.

- Use the category that most effectively shows the research done.

- Be selective in what is included in the bibliography. Limit the annotations to two sentences except for truly exceptional sources. Primary source annotations should explain why the source is primary to the topic.

- A professional appearance in an Exhibit or a Documentary is essential. Use the best technology available, but don't overdo the special effects. Clarity is the key.

- Be meticulous about citing sources and giving credit for illustrations, graphics, music, and artifacts. This includes identifying the sponsors of websites used in research or for illustrative material.

- When handling controversial issues, make sure the nature of the disagreement is clear, the core issues are identified, and the focus is on ideas instead of personalities.

- Check and double-check the paperwork. Errors in spelling or grammar make a very bad impression.

- "Balanced research" means showing both sides of an issue AND using a wide variety of sources.

- Whatever the category, the narrative should flow. Don't interrupt the story with excessive quotes or statistics. Use only what is appropriate and effective.

- Show a present day result or legacy of the topic if it's accurate and appropriate, but don't stretch the analysis with broad generalizations.

- Use the vocabulary of the annual theme whenever appropriate (in captions or script, bibliography annotations, interview responses, etc.).

- Revisit the suggestions in The Annotated Bibliography, Helpful Hints for Winning Projects, Interview Dos and Don'ts, and the Hints handout for the specific category. All are found in the Student Research and Presentation section.

Some Advice from a Winner

The following advice is from a NHD finalist in the
Junior Individual Exhibits category in 1999.

- Be sure to check for available sources before deciding on a topic.

- You need to be dedicated. Plan to spend a lot of time in libraries.

- Every project needs order and focus. Use subtitles to organize the story.

- Use quotes, songs, ads, or poems to give color, feel, and character to your story. On an Exhibit board the words don't count toward the 500 word limit of "student generated" text.

- Learn to use a thesaurus.

- Don't offend anyone!

- Have a variety of people look at, watch, or read your project and critique it. Be open to suggestions for improvement, but remember you don't have to use them all.

- After each level of competition evaluate the judges' comments carefully. Follow through on any suggestions of sources to check or people to contact.

- When writing the captions, script, or Process Narrative, say what you want first, then edit down to word or time limit. Make sure that the focus is maintained when cuts are made.

- Size of print for Exhibits or Documentaries should be legible from a reasonable distance. Size of print in the Process Narrative and Annotated Bibliography should be no larger that 14 point or it fails to appear serious.

- Use the time between contests to do the little things you didn't have time for before.

- Take an "emergency kit" to the contest. This should contain extra copies of your paperwork and replacement parts for anything that can easily break or be lost, plus any tools you might need for on-the-spot repairs.

Regional History Fair Participants

1. Regional History Fair competition is on _____ at _____.

2. _____ History Department will provide transportation on _____ for students to set up Exhibits and for the Documentary and Performance projects to present. Parents must arrange for transportation on _____ for the Awards Ceremony and to remove Exhibits.

3. The _____ ISD/school will/will not pay the registration fee.

4. Papers must be submitted by _____ and Paper writers need only be present at the Awards Ceremony.

5. Students must be willing to:

   A. Rework the project—board, paper, performance, or documentary.

   B. Add primary sources to the research and expand as much as possible in the time available.

   C. Make sure the theme: "_____

   _____ "

   is really obvious both in presentation and in paperwork.

   D. Follow all rules to the letter. All students should have a copy of the official *National History Day Rule Book*. Copies can be obtained from _____ in room _____.

   E. Make sure all written material is proofed by an English teacher—no errors allowed.

6. Please let _____ know for sure if you are entering Regional competition by _____ at _____ AM/PM. You may change anything EXCEPT your topic and your category. Please advise title or group changes ASAP. (Once registration papers are submitted, titles cannot be changed nor can group members be dropped.)

7. Please don't be embarrassed to drop out if you don't have time to do this, or you really are not that interested. Now is better than later.

8. If you have any problems or questions please contact _____ at/in _____.

(date)

Dear Parent,

Your child is registered to compete in the _____ Regional History Fair at _____ on _____. We will send _____ projects done by _____ students. This is an excellent showing and I believe we can come home with some prizes, maybe even send a project or two on to State competition.

All projects need to be expanded and improved as much as possible before Regional competition. In addition, all rules must be followed to the letter so as not to be disqualified for a rule violation. Students have approximately _____ weeks to work. If field trips or interviews are planned, arrange to do them as soon as possible.

On _____ afternoon, _____, there will be a History Fair information session in the school library for students going to Regional and their parents. Please join us if you can. We will show slides of exemplary Exhibits, discuss rules, and answer questions. Your student may bring the project and/or required paperwork to discuss if he or she wishes. The three main things to concentrate on are: good solid research, primary sources, and theme.

The History Department is arranging for a bus to take students and their projects to _____ on _____. You will receive a permission form closer to that date. On _____ students with Exhibits will set them up in their designated area, while students doing Performances or Documentaries will present for the judges. (Papers, of course, are submitted before the competition to give judges plenty of time to read them.) We will return to campus when all contestants have finished. The Exhibits are judged on _____. Parents and other visitors may view the projects beginning at _____ on _____ and the Awards Ceremony starts at _____ AM/PM. Parents are responsible for transportation to and from the Awards program and all Exhibits must be removed from the display area by _____ AM/PM.

We are absolutely thrilled with the quality of our projects and are looking forward to working with the students as they prepare for Regional. We met many of you at the History Fair Open House and hope to see you again on _____. If you cannot be there, or have questions or concerns, please do not hesitate to call the school at _____. We appreciate your support.

Sincerely,

_____
History Fair Director

History Fair
Out-of-Town Competition Travel Permission
and Parent Release

I, _____ give _____, my
     (Print parent or guardian name)   (Print student name)

son/daughter/ward permission to travel to _____ with
                                                      (location)

_____, chaperone/sponsor, for _____ History
    (Print teacher/coach name)   (level)

Fair competition, leaving on _____ at _____ AM/PM
                                (date)   (time)

and returning on _____ at _____ AM/PM.
                          (date)   (time)

As my student is representing _____ School at the event described above, I understand and support the following conditions:

- All school and district rules regarding student conduct remain in effect for the entire trip and will be enforced.

- I will provide my child with money for _____

   _____.

- Any student who displays disruptive or detrimental behavior, including the possession or being under the influence of alcohol or illegal drugs, will be immediately withdrawn from the program and returned to his or her parents, with probable school disciplinary action to follow.

- Students are not allowed to carry prescription drugs or other medications while on this trip. Therefore, I have given the chaperone/sponsor named above any regular or as-needed medication for my child and attached specific instructions for its administration. In addition, I have also attached a detailed account of any special medical problem or need my child has. (Items attached Yes/No ?)
                                          (Circle one)

I hereby release _____ School and the _____ School District and its employees from any liability for my child while he/she is taking part in this event. Nor will I hold the school, the district or the sponsor(s) responsible for any injury or other loss occurring during the trip and related activities, or any conditions resulting from my child's failure to follow the instructions of the sponsoring teacher(s). Furthermore, I authorize the sponsoring teacher(s) named above to execute all documents necessary for my child to be treated by a medical doctor or at a medical facility should such a need arise for his or her care and general welfare.

Signed _____ Date _____
                (Signature of Parent or Guardian)

Emergency Phone_____ Alternate contact: _____

139

(date)

Mr. and Mrs. Perfect Parent
122 Schoolhouse Lane
Anytown USA

Dear Mr. and Mrs. Parent,

I want you to know how very much I enjoyed working with _____ on the History Fair project this year. As a teacher, I have been very fortunate to occasionally encounter students who are talented and dedicated enough to succeed at State and National competitions. _____ was one of those few. You have every reason to be extremely proud of your daughter/son.

I also want to thank you for your continued support of both the History Fair program and the *(insert title)* project. Without parental support and encouragement students have a very difficult time achieving the kind of honors _____ received. Please continue to take an active part in her/his education and make sure she/he knows you value her/his success.

_____ has a bright and challenging future ahead of her/him as she/he enters high school. This is going to be a year of really big changes. I know her/his History Fair experience will give her/him confidence and skills which she/he will find very useful these next few years. In addition, I sincerely hope she/he will use this year as a beginning and continue in the History Fair program with another project. Whether that happens or not, I know that what she/he has learned this year will benefit her/him in whatever future she/he chooses.

Again, thank you for the opportunity to coach _____ in History Fair. Working with her/him has been a pleasure and a reward for me.

Sincerely,

_____
History Fair Director

VIII. Appendixes

Correlation of Objectives and Standards
National History Day and National Council for the Social Studies

NHD Student Objectives	NCSS Essential Skills for Social Studies	NCSS Standards in Historical Thinking
• Develop research and reading skills and refine presentation skills in writing, visual projects, and performances.	• Read for a variety of purposes, read various forms of printed material.	• Obtain historical data.
• Develop critical-thinking and problem-solving skills that will help students manage and use information effectively now and in the future.	• Present visually information extracted from print.	• Formulate historical questions.
• Integrate the materials and methods of social studies, art, literature, language, and music into their entries.	• Detect cause-and-effect relationships, distinguish between fact and opinion, recognize propaganda, recognize author bias.	• Evidence historical perspectives.
• Express themselves creatively through presentations of historical topics and materials in a variety of formats.	• Make an outline, prepare summaries, make timelines, take notes, prepare a bibliography.	• Utilize visual and mathematical data.
• Develop a sense of history as process and change, a multifaceted development over time that affects every aspect of human life and society.	• Test the validity of information.	• Interrogate historical data.
• Get students out of the school building and into the community, investigating local history.	• Use literature to enrich meaning.	• Analyze cause-and-effect relationships and multiple causation, including the importance of the individual.
	• Use appropriate sources of information.	• Differentiate between historical facts and historical interpretation.
	• Form an opinion based on critical examination of relevant information.	• Compare and contrast differing sets of ideas, (or) values.
	• Restate major ideas of a complex topic.	• Consider multiple perspectives.
	• Communicate orally and in writing.	• Draw upon visual, literary, and musical scores.
	• Recognize the values implicit in situations and the issues that flow from them.	• Construct a sound historical interpretation.
	• Recognize the mutual relationship between human beings in satisfying one another's needs.	• Reconstruct the literal meaning of a historical passage.
	• Use the community as a resource.	• Establish temporal order in historical narratives.
	• Use sources of information in the community, conduct interviews, use community newspapers.	• Identify issues and problems in the past.
	• Interpret history through artifacts.	• Identify relevant historical antecedents.
		• Compare competing historical narratives.
		• Reconstruct patterns of historical succession and duration.
		• Identify gaps in existing records.
		• Marshal evidence of antecedent circumstances and contemporary factors contributing to problems and alternative courses of action.

(Adapted from: "What is National History Day?" *National History Day 1998: Migration in History.* NHD 1998 Curriculum Book, p. 5)

(Adapted from: National Council for the Social Studies, *Curriculum Standards for Social Studies.* Washington, DC, 1994, Appendix A.)

(Adapted from: Gale, Mark. "Meeting the Standards: NHD in Today's Classroom." NHD published pamphlet, 2000.)

PRIMARY SOURCE COLLECTIONS
(Especially useful for school libraries)

The Annals of America (21 vols.) Chicago: Encyclopedia Britannica, 1976.

Album of American History (4 vols.) Charles Scribner's Sons. (pictures)

American Historical Images on File (5 vols.) New York: Facts On File. (portraits)

Bigelow, Barbara C. *World War II Primary Sources*. Detroit: UXL, 2000.

Commager, Henry Steele, ed. *Documents of American History*. New York: Appleton-Century-Crofts, 1968.

An Eyewitness History (Series) New York: Facts On File.

Engelbert, Phillis. *American Civil Rights Primary Sources*. Detroit: UXL, 1999.

Friedman, Ina R., ed. *The Other Victims: First-Person Stories of Non-Jews Persecuted by the Nazis*. Boston: Houghton Mifflin, 1990.

Gregory, Ross, ed. *Almanacs of American Life* (3 vols.) New York: Facts On File, 1995.

Hillstrom, Kevin, and Laurie Collier Hillstrom. *American Civil War Primary Sources*. Detroit: UXL, 2000.

Knight, Judson. *Slavery throughout History Primary Sources*. Detroit: UXL, 2000.

Monk, Linda R., ed. *Ordinary Americans: U.S. History through the Eyes of Everyday People*. Alexandria, VA: Close Up Publishing, 1994.

Perspectives in History (series) Discovery Enterprises. (individual booklets, all primary sources, over 75 titles)

Podell, Janet, and Steven Anzovin, eds. *Speeches of the American Presidents*. New York: H.W. Wilson, 1988.

Rae, Noel, ed. *Witnessing America*. New York: Stonesong Press Book, 1996.

Saari, Peggy. *Colonial America Primary Sources*. Detroit: UXL, 2000.

Schlissel, Lillian. *Women's Diaries of the Westward Journey*. New York: Schocken Books, 1982.

Schmittroth, Linda. *American Revolution Primary Sources*. Detroit: UXL, 2000.

Teaching with Primary Sources series from Cobblestone Publishing Company. (individual titles such as *The American Frontier, The Civil War, The Immigrant Experience, Seneca Falls*, etc., in binder format)

Toll, Nelly S., *Behind the Secret Window: A Memoir of a Hidden Childhood During World War II*. New York: Dial Books, 1993.

Twentieth Century America (10 vols) New York: Grolier Educational Corporation, 1995.

Resources

1. **National History Day**
   - Website <www.nationalhistoryday.org>
   - Names and addresses of State History Day Coordinators
   - NHD Institutes for teachers: one week in the summer, others as announced, focus is on coming year's theme and use of primary sources in the classroom. Twenty-five participants, expenses at Institute paid.
   - Join H-HistoryDay e-mail discussion listserv for teachers, parents, and other adults involved in History Fair.
   - Complete list of NHD winners from the most recent competition.
   - Suggested topic list for the upcoming year's theme.
   - Bibliography information for students.
   - For several weeks before the National History Day competition, while students from all over the country are registering for the event, participants can check the status of their registration and the titles of their competition.
   - Order *Rule Book*, Judging forms, annual *Curriculum Book*, and other materials from:
     > National History Day
     > 0119 Cecil Hall
     > University of Maryland
     > College Park, MD 20742
     > phone: 301-314-9739

2. **Teacher Materials and Ideas**
   - *Jackdaws* are primary source packets on individual topics. Numerous titles available from Jackdaws, Division of Golden Owl Publishing, P.O. Box 503, Anawalk, NJ 10501.
   - Minnesota Historical Society. History Day, MHS Education, 345 Kellogg Blvd. West, St. Paul, MN 55102-1906. 651-284-3817, Fax 651-282-2484. Video tapes of Documentary and Performance projects, slides of Exhibits (all National finalists) and other teacher materials.
   - Organization of American Historians' *Magazine of History* usually publishes an annual issue focused on the upcoming National History Day theme. This is a journal for secondary teachers that includes both articles and lesson plans, most featuring primary documents.
   - Weitzman, David. *My Backyard History Book.*. Boston: Little, Brown, 1975. Many ideas on local and family history.
   - Bettmann, Otto L. *The Good Days—They Were Terrible!* New York: Random House, 1974. Wonderful topic ideas and fascinating illustrations.
   - Also see the Bibliography of Primary Source Collections in this appendix.

3. **Sources for Teacher/Student/Parent**
   - National Archives and Records Administration's "Digital Classroom" at <www.nara.gov/education> has lessons, ideas and links for current NHD theme. The Online Exhibit Hall has posters, photos, documents at <www.nara.gov/exhall/exhibits.html> The Regional Records Service Facilities at <http://www.nara.gov/regional/nrmenu.html> lists resources at branches in Alaska, California, Colorado, Georgia, Illinois, Massachusetts, Missouri, New York, Ohio, Pennsylvania, Texas and Washington State.
   - American Memory Project: see a full list of over seventy collections at <http://memory.loc.gov/ammen/amhome.html> A companion Learning Page provides lesson ideas and activities. Under Research Tools find hints for History Fair projects.

- American Association for State and Local History
    1717 Church Street
    Nashville, TN 37203
    phone: 615-320-3203
    web: <www.aaslh.org>
- Oral History Association
    Dickinson College
    P.O. Box 1773
    Carlisle, PA 17013
    phone: 717-245-1036
    web: <http://dickinson.edu.oha>
- Turabian, Kate L. *A Manual for Writers of Term Papers, Theses, and Dissertations*, Sixth edition. Chicago: University of Chicago Press, 1996.

4. Supplies

- Educational Products, Inc.
    1342 North IH 35 East, Dallas, TX 75006
    1-800-365-5345, 214-245-9512, Fax 214-245-5632
    Exhibit boards, Prize ribbons, Certificates, Buttons, other contest items.
- William K. Sheridan and Associates
    8311 Greenmeadows Dr. North
    Lewis Center, Ohio, 43035
    1-800-433-6259, 614-548-0575, Fax 614-548-0485
    Exhibit boards and Awards
- Atlas R-Board (or R-Max) is a sturdy, light-weight fiberglass siding insulation. It can be used for exhibit panels, can be framed with corner molding, and takes straight pins. Available at home improvement centers.
- Unbleached cotton muslin, available at any fabric store in various widths, makes excellent cover for exhibit boards as well as backdrops for performances.
- Rubber cement used as adhesive on exhibit boards allows for items to be moved and repositioned without leaving marks. It also works well for mounting illustrations or captions as it does not wrinkle white copy paper as it dries.
- Glue guns are easy and practical, but permanent. Good for last minute or emergency repairs.
- Velcro strips or patches have a variety of applications for project assembly. They can be found in white or black, one sided (two strips make a pair) or double sided (can form a loop and stick to itself).

Sample Title Page
(for all competitions beyond campus fair)

The Great Emancipator:
Abe Lincoln Takes a Stand
(title)

Susan Student
and
Carlos Competitor
(name or names)

Junior Group Documentary
(division)   *(category)*

_____

(May be asked to write project number here.)

(Use plain white paper with black print, no decoration, illustration, border, or cover of any kind.)

The two papers included here are examples of the Process Narrative. Both projects were National History Day finalists. Paper #1 is from 1999 when the theme was "Science, Technology, and Invention: Impact, Influence, and Change."

1.

A STITCH IN TIME:

THE THREAD OF TECHNOLOGY

(6th place, Junior Individual Exhibits)

The sewing machine is one of the greatest technological inventions of all time. It was among the first home appliances in the American Industrial Revolution. It influenced the role and status of women, revolutionized the garment trade, and modernized other businesses such as shoemaking and upholstery. The ability of women to produce clothing faster and more efficiently increased the wardrobe each family member could own. Whether in the home or factory, the sewing machine replaced the tedious work of hand sewing. By 1890 some 110,000 sewing machines were being manufactured and sold in the United States annually.

The sewing machine fits the theme "Science, Technology, and Invention in History: Impact, Influence, and Change" perfectly because it developed through the influence of many inventors. It impacted the lives and work of seamstresses, tailors, and shoemakers. It influenced the development of the American ready-to-wear industry and changed the way clothing is produced. I chose the sewing machine as my project because of my personal interest in sewing and in clothing. Both my grandmother and great-grandmother have been sewing all their lives—both out of necessity and for their own enjoyment.

My Project was developed through many personal interviews, library research, and Internet sources. At a sewing convention in San Antonio I had the opportunity to interview a PBS television personality who has her own sewing show. We talked about the impact of the sewing machine on society. During the development of my project I visited a factory where sewing machines are used to make flags and banners, and another where clothing is made. I watched while leather upholstery was sewn together to make seat covers, and later observed seamstresses making alterations on clothing.

My most memorable interview was with a seventy-nine-year-old gentleman who makes custom-made boots. He learned to sew at the age of nine because he had no one to repair the holes in his pants. His dream was to make and repair shoes and have the best sewing machines available. He owns his own store today and has a wide variety of sewing machines.

People used to think sewing machines would put seamstresses out of work. What really happened is the same as what happened with the computer: Instead of eliminating jobs, it raised expectations. The new technology changed the role of the worker only to make the job more efficient, reducing time and cost, but then people wanted more. Today, factory use of the sewing machine is international. From clothing to shoes and upholstery and luggage, the sewing machine makes possible the things we wear and use.

My exhibit outlines how the sewing machine was invented, how advertising and marketing changed to promote this new invention, and how it impacted both home and factory sewers. In the 19th century it was said, "a woman who cannot sew is as deficient as a man who cannot write." Certainly this is no longer true. Today the sewing machine makes it possible for both men and women to own extensive wardrobes. It is truly the thread of technology.

2.

"YOUR OLD MAN'S A MONKEY"

THE SCOPES TRIAL

(3rd place, Junior Individual Documentaries)

I began thinking about this project almost a year ago. My family was discussing interesting but unusual history fair topics. Although I had heard of the Scopes Trial, I didn't know much about it or think I could find enough information about it. The Scopes Trial was a fascinating topic, and was a frontier in history due to the issues raised. The Scopes Trial made people stop and think about their beliefs. It made Americans, instead of just the scientists of the day, seriously consider evolution. It pushed the topic forward into the spotlight. The subjects examined in the trial remain controversial issues even today.

I started researching my topic to get background information. For this, I went to my school library and got a biography of Clarence Darrow with a small section on the Scopes Trial, and a basic book about the trial. These helped me to understand the main points of the trial. I needed more information before I could consider doing interviews and putting my project together. I tried the Internet. I found many sites, the best being a UMKC School of Law web page. There was an entire section dedicated to famous American trials, one being the Scopes Trial. I also found some information on the American Atheist site. It talked about how the church vs. state debate continues today. Then I went to the Central San Antonio Public Library to check out several books. All of them were helpful, especially one by Edward J. Larson, *Summer for the Gods*. I read about the movie *Inherit the Wind*, loosely based on the Scopes Trial. I later interviewed the priests from my church, a nondenominational minister, a Jewish Federation spokeswoman, and a fundamentalist minister for their opinions on evolution vs. creationism, and church vs. state. I interviewed two teachers about the educational implications raised by the trial. I talked to an attorney about the legal aspects of the case. I also interviewed my great aunt Marian and grandfather for historical perspective.

The Scopes Trial was a frontier in many ways, opening up public debate over separation of church and state as well as evolution. It made people think literally about creation. Who's right: The scientists or the fundamentalists? It was a trial over the freedom of speech and the freedom of religion. The defenders believed the trial was about the right to think beyond the Bible. The prosecutors believed it was a personal attack against God and the Bible. In the end, it pushed the view of the nation and the world to science and the creation of man, an important step in education and the country's history. As one book put it, "It raised a fundamental question about the nature of education" (Grant, Robert, and Joseph Katz. *The Great Trials of the Twenties*, p. 154). For a trial based on a narrow point of law, the Scopes trial opened up broad discussions that continue today.

Topics
"Science, Technology, and Invention in History: Impact, Influence, Change"
(NHD theme for 1999)

I. American History

Telephone, Alexander Graham Bell
Telegraph, Samuel B. Morse
Sanitation, indoor plumbing, sewers, John Crapper
Samuel Slater, Moses Brown (first textile mills in U.S.)
Brooklyn Bridge, Golden Gate Bridge, also tunnels
Alfred Nobel, dynamite
Transcontinental Railroad, locomotives, trains
Robert Fulton, steamboat
Sewing machine, Elias Howe, Issac Singer
Springfield Armory (made guns for the US Army)
Winchester Rifle, Colt revolver, other classic guns
Cyrus McCormick, farm machines
Eli Whitney, interchangeable parts
Cotton gin, invention, also Slavery connection
Eleanor Butterick, home sewing dress patterns
18th century "How To" books
Child Labor in textile mills, mines, other industry
Water Power, steam power
Women's Work, domestic technology, 17th–20th cent.
Mary Baker Eddy, Christian Science Church
Matthew Brady, Civil War photography
Medicine, anesthetics, surgery, field hospitals
Ironclads, Merrimack and Monitor (Civil War)
Wright Bros., airplane, air travel,
Helicopters (first used in Korean War)
Automobile, Henry Ford, assembly line
Highways, National Highway System, Interstate Hwys.
Billy Mitchell, air warfare
Television and the Vietnam War
NOAA, National Weather Service
Dr. Benjamin Spock, the "baby doctor"
Walt Disney, "imagineering"
Skyscrapers, Empire State Building, Otis elevators
Hollerith, punchcard tabulating, US Census
Spindletop, Oil Industry, Red Adair, Alaska Pipeline
Scopes "Monkey" Trial (Evolution lost in Tennessee)
Modern packaged foods: Campbell's soup, Spam, etc.
Nutrition, discovery and use of vitamins
George Washington Carver, new food plants and uses
Cartography: aerial mapping, sattelites, GIS, computers
Architecture, Frank Lloyd Wright
Rosie the Riveter, women's work in WWII
Tennessee Valley Authority project: dam, electric plant
Rural Electrification project
Forensics, Crime detection, fingerprints, DNA

Mortuary science (Lincoln first pres. to be embalmed)
Atomic Bomb, Manhattan Project, R. Oppenheimer
Computers, Grace Hopper, Bill Gates, IBM, Apple
Frederick Taylor, efficiency in industrial management
Breakingthe sound barrier, jet airplanes, Chuck Yeager
Radio, TV, Internet technology
Thomas Edison, electric light bulb, many inventions
Movies, film industry, Hollywood, special effects
USDA, meat, food safety
Erie Canal, Panama Canal, other canals

II. World History

Castles, walls, war engines, catapult, siege techniques
Calendars: Mayan, Aztec, Roman, medieval
Inca Empire, roads, cities, plumbing, surgery
Egyptian science and technology
Alchemists, Francis Bacon
Gunpowder
Medieval Guilds
Leonardo da Vinci
Albert Einstein
Chimney, other early architectural developments
Astronomy, Copernicus, Galileo, Telescopes
Clocks, timekeeping
Latitude, Longitude, John Harrison
Printing press, Johann Gutenberg
Anton VanLeeuwenhoek, microscope
Charles Darwin, evolution and natural selection
Photography, tintypes, George Eastman, Kodak
Lloyd's of London, insurance (especially maritime ins.)
Ballooning; Windmills
Louis Braille, Braille typewriter, Braille books
Guillotine (French Revolution)
Diderot encyclopedia of technology
Luddites (anti-technology movement in England)
Iron, steel, Darby, Bessemer
Scientific instruments (see collection at Harvard Univ.)
Luxury liners: Titanic, Queen Mary, QEII
Vaccines: smallpox, measles, cholera, polio, etc.
Espionage technology
Jacques Cousteau, aqualung, explorations
Submarines, tanks, RADAR, torpedo, other war tech.
Modern archaeology, discoveries, hoaxes
Codes and code-breaking in WWI and WWII, Enigma machine, Navajo Code-talkers, etc.

Please use this list for ideas. You are NOT limited to these topics. Always check with your teacher.

Topics
"Turning Points in History: People, Events, Ideas"
(NHD theme for 2000)

I. American History

Battle of Midway, WWII, Pacific
Puritans come to America for religious freedom, 1620
Chuck Yeager breaks the sound barrier (c. 1947)
Rosa Parks, other Civil Rights leaders and events
Robert Moses redesigns New York City
Battle of Saratoga, American Revolution
Rifle, Gatlin gun, other "first" weapons
Shay's Rebellion, reason for U.S. Constitution, 1786
The Dawes Act (Homesteads, RR land, Reservations)
Voting Rights Act of 1965
Alamo, Battle in 1836, Texas Independence
Babe Zaharias, women in sports, Title IX
Sally Ride, women astronauts
Plessy vs. Ferguson, "separate but equal" decision, 1899
Joe McCarthy, anti-communist witch hunt, 1950s
Tennessee Valley Authority, electric power project
Rural electrification in 1930s
Roe vs. Wade, abortion legalized, 1974
Brown vs. Board of Education, school integration, 1954
Trans-Continental Railroad, first completed in 1869
Oberlin College (Ohio) first co-ed university in U.S.
Mormons establish home in Utah, 1848
Ready-to-wear clothes: men c. 1866; women c. 1900
Issac Singer, first practical sewing machine, 1852
Synthetic fertilizers, explosives, Alfred Nobel
Closing of the American Frontier (1890)
Marquis de LaFayette comes to America (Amer. Revol.)
Louisiana Purchase, Lewis and Clark Expedition
FDR and the New Deal, Social Security, other programs
Manhattan Project, Atomic Bomb, end of WWII
Battle of Gettysburg (Civil War)
Samuel Slater/Slater Mill, first U.S. factory, 1790
Elvis Presley, revolution in American popular music
Kent State, VietNam War protesters (students) killed
Automobile changes American life
Henry Ford perfects the assembly line
Eli Whitney, cotton gin, interchangeable parts
Nylon, Armstrong, DuPont Chemicals, 1930s
Clara Barton, American Red Cross (after Civil War)
Seneca Falls Convention, Women's Suffrage Movement
Personal computers, Internet
Grace Hopper, COBOL, computer language for business
Miranda Decision ("reading you your rights")
Dred Scott decision ("once a slave, always a slave")
Fugitive Slave Law, 1850, and *Uncle Tom's Cabin*

Panama Canal
Apollo 11, Moon Walk, 1969
Chinese Exclusion Act (first immigration quotas)
Television, 1939 World's Fair, Philo Farnsworth
WACs in WWII, Ovetta Culp Hobby
Endangered Species Act
"The Pill" (oral contraception for women), 1960s
Watergate scandal and resignation of Richard Nixon
Lusitania, sinking by Germany brings U.S. into WWI
Sputnik, USSR launches first satellite, 1957
Radio Free Europe, American propaganda in Cold War

II. World History

Nelson Mandela, end of Apartheid in South Africa
Martin Luther, Protestant Reformation, Germany, 1517
Industrial Revolution, England, 1700s
Gunpowder, introduction in Europe
Hiroshima, post-war Japan
Sigmund Freud, beginning of psychoanalysis
Iron Curtain, Cold War
Mexican Revolution, 1910-20, Zapata, Villa, Carranza
D-Day (June 6, 1944) Allied invasion of Europe, WWII
Marco Polo returns from China, 1200s
Mt. Vesuvius, destruction of Pompei
Black Death (Bubonic Plague), Europe 1348-52
St. Paul, spread of Christianity to non-Jewish world
Mohammed/Islam, conversion by conquest, 600s AD
Dr. Leakey in Africa (finding the earliest humans)
Bolshevik Revolution, beginning of USSR, 1917
Magna Carta, 1215 AD, first written constitution
Columbus, first European contact with Americas
Hernan Cortes, conquest of the Aztecs, 1521
Galileo (paradign shift—sun as center of the universe)
Defeat of the Spanish Armada, 1588
Watson and Crick, discovery of DNA
Beatles ("the British Invasion")
Geneva Convention (war rules, prisoners-of-war, etc.)
Berlin Airlift, Berlin Wall
Adm. Lord Nelson, Battle of Trafalgar (vs. French)
Norman Conquest of Britain, 1066
Venerable Bede, first "modern" historian
Cinco de Mayo, French defeated in Mexico, 1860s
Solidarity movement in Poland, Lech Walesa
Alexander the Great conquers the known world
Charlemagne and the Holy Roman Empire

Please use this list for ideas. You are NOT limited to these topics. Always check with your teacaher.

Topics
"Frontiers in History: People, Places, Ideas"
(NHD theme for 2001)

I. American History

Mail order companies, Sears and Roebuck, Mont. Ward
Frontier women: Jamestown, Kentucky, wagon trains
Utopian communities (e.g., Post, Texas)
American West, wagon trains, Pony Express
Transcontinental Railroad, first one completed 1869
Wright Brothers, first flight at Kittyhawk, NC, 1903
Fur traders, French coureur de bois, mountain men
California Gold Rush of 1849, also Colorado, Klondike
Cattle drives, ended by railroads and barbed wire
NASA , space as the new frontier
Spanish borderlands and Spanish missions
Robert Fulton, steam boat
Henry Ford, assembly line
New Deal, government aid programs, Great Depression
Women's Suffrage Movement, Seneca Falls, 1848
Civil Rights Movement, numerous topics
Dorothea Dix, reformer of prisons and mental hospitals
Mormons settle in Utah, 1848
Elvis Presley, Bob Dylan, frontiers in American music
Radio, television, telephone, communication frontiers
Frank Lloyd Wright, pioneer in American architecture
Elizabeth Blackwell, first female doctor
Homestead Act and the Dawes Act (Indian reservations)
Atomic bomb/Atomic energy, frontiers in power
Oklahoma Territory land rush, "sooners," 1889
Louisiana Purchase, Lewis and Clark expedition
John Dewey, educational reform, public education
Weatherill, archaeology/anthropology of southwest U.S.
1848 Mexican War, Treaty of Guadalupe Hidalgo
Zebulon Pike, explorer, Pike's Peak
John Butterfield, Wells Fargo, frontier transportation
Albany Plan of Union, attempt to unite 13 colonies
American Colonization Society, freed slaves to Liberia
Orphan Trains
American Temperance Society, figting alcohol abuse
John Jacob Astor, settling the Oregon Territory
John James Audubon, documenting wildlife
Thirteen English colonies, each a different frontier story
Amelia Earhart, women in aviation
Daniel Boone, trans-Appalachain west, Kentucky
Spindletop, first oilfield (near Beaumont, Texas)
Irish come to America, 1840s
Robert LaSalle, explored Great Lakes, Mississippi River
Christian Church on the frontier, circuit riders
Oregon Trail, Santa Fe Trail, other routes west

II. World History

Watson and Crick, discovery of DNA
Colonialism, European colonies in Africa and Asia
Martin Luther, Protestant Reformation, 1500s
Muslim conquest of N. Africa, Middle East, and Spain
Walls as defense of frontier: Hadrian's Wall in England,
the Great Wall of China, Berlin Wall, others
Cold War, the Iron Curtain, N/S Korea, N/S Vietnam
Capitalism vs. Communism, frontiers in economics
Medici, Renaissance banking begins in Italy
Mexican Revolution of 1910–1920
Democracy in ancient Greece, Rome
Parliaments, development of modern government
Gandhi in India, social reforms, non-violent protest
Israel, ancient and modern, many frontier topics
D-Day, World War II, many related topics
Norman (French) Conquest of England, 1066
Cortes in Mexico; Pizarro in Peru; Perry in Japan
Jacques Cousteau, underwater frontiers
Franciscans, Dominicans, missionaries in the Americas
Iceland/Greenland to North America, Viking frontiers
Darwin, evolution and natural selection
Bible, translation, printing (e.g., King James' in 1600s)
Magna Carta, English Bill of Rights
Ottoman Empire, the Berlin-to-Bagdad Railroad
Venerable Bede, early English historian
Bolshevik Revolution, Russia becomes USSR
British East India Company; Hudson Bay Company
Portuguese colonization of Brazil
Ferdinand and Isabel, uniting Spain in the 1400s
Roman Empire frontier provinces, Spain, France, Britain
Greek/Roman colonization of the Mediterranean
Holy Land (Isarel) as Christian frontier during Crusades
Early civilization, beginning of agriculture
Charlemagne and the Holy Roman Empire
Alexander the Great, Persian Empire
Development of alphabet, beginning of written language
Columbus discovers America
Vasco da Gama discovers sea route around Africa
Medical frontiers: antibiotics, anesthesia, vaccines
Aztecs settle in Mexico, build an empire
Bering Strait migration (early humans come to America)
Geoffrey Chaucer (first to write literature in English)
St.Patrick, taking Christian religion to Ireland
League of Nations, United Nations

Please use this list for ideas. You are NOT limited to these topics. Always check with your teacher.

Topics
"Revolution, Reaction, and Reform in History"
(NHD theme for 2002)

I. American History
Red Scare, Palmer Raids (1920s)
House Un-American Affairs Committee (Cold War)
National Security Act of 1948 (reform of the military)
Hippies/anti-war movement, Kent State, 1960s
Martin Luther King, Malcolm X, Civil Rights leaders
Henry Ford, assembly line, revolution in manufacturing
Rachel Carson, *Silent Spring*, reaction to pollution
Environmental movement, Sierra Club, Greenpeace
Nat Turner, slave rebellion, 1830s
Carrie Nation, Women's Christian Temperance Union
Horace Mann, reform of public education
Miranda Act, reform of police policy toward accused
Ku Klux Klan as reaction to the abolition of slavery
Mail Order merchandising, Sears, Montgomery Ward
Abolitionists/Anti-Slavery movement, Douglass, Brown
Jane Addams, settlement houses for immigrants
Great Awakening, 18th century religious movement
Jackson presidency, first "common man" president
Freedom Riders, 1960s Civil Rights Movement
Industrial Revolution, many topics
FDR's New Deal, reform during Great Depression
Emancipation Proclamation (1863)
Women's suffrage, feminism, Equal Rights Amend.
Transportation revolutions: steamship, railroads,
automobiles, airplanes
Invention of typewriter, women in the work force
Brown vs. Board of Education, school desegregation
Texas independence from Mexico, the Alamo (1836)
Margaret Sanger, reformer and pioneer in birth control
Title IX (reform of education for gender equality)
Pueblo Uprising, New Mexico, 1600s
Ralph Nader, reform in consumer protection
Dorothea Dix, reform of mental hospitals and prisons
Martha Graham, revolution in Modern Dance
John Peter Zenger, early American freedom of the press
Right-to-Life movement as reaction to Roe v. Wade
Columbian Exchange, revolution in nutrition and culture
Jazz, revolutionary American music
Japanese internment, WWII, reaction to Pearl Harbor
Tecumseh, Indian reaction to American expansion
Dawes Act, Bureau of Indian Affairs, reservations
Clara Barton, American Red Cross, reform in nursing
Margaret Meade, revolutionary anthropologist
Bonus Army, WWI veterans' protest
Harriet Beecher Stowe, *Uncle Tom's Cabin*, 1852

II. World History
"Troubles" in Ireland, IRA, SinnFein
Parnell, Irish Independence movement
Mexican Revolution, 1910–1920, Villa, Zapata
"Grito de Dolores," Fr. Hidalgo, Mexican independence
Mohammed, beginning of Islam (600s AD)
Haiti, Toussaint L'Ouverture (slaves win independence)
Coco Chanel, Christian Dior, French designers
Protestant Reformation, Martin Luther, 1500s
Counter Reformation (Catholic reaction to Luther)
Gutenberg and the printing press
Medici, Italian Renaissance revolution in banking
Copernicus, Galileo, Kepler, revolution in astronomy
Berlin Wall, built in Cold War, destroyed 1991
Soviet Union, fall of communism, Yeltsin (1991)
Poland, Solidarity workers' union
Vatican Council II, modern reform of Catholic Church
Bolshevik Revolution, beginning of Soviet Union
Cuba, Fidel Castro (communist take-over 1960)
Opium Wars, Boxer Rebellion (China, early 1900s)
Luddites, reaction against textile technology in Britain
Vietnam, revolution against colonialism
Warsaw Ghetto in WWII, Polish Jews resist Nazi control
India, independence, Gandhi, non-violent protest
John Wesley, founder of Methodist Church, reformer
Apartheid in South Africa, Nelson Mandela, Bishop Tutu
Benito Juarez revolts against French rule in Mexico
Medieval monastic reform, Francis of Assisi, Cluny
Simón Bolivar, José Martí, Latin American liberators
French Revolution, Reign of Terror, Napoleon Bonaparte
Hitler/Nazi Party as reaction to Treaty of Versailles
Oliver Cromwell and the English Civil War (1600s)
English Restoration, reaction to Puritan rule (1600s)
Mao Tse Tung, Chiang Kai Shek, Communist revolt
Pablo Picasso, revolutionary art, 20th century
Nasser, Pan-Arab Nationalism, reaction to Imperialism
Magna Carta, 1215, revolution in limited government
Tibet, revolt against Chinese oppression, Dalai Lama
Charles Darwin, revolution and reaction in science
Florence Nightengale (British nurse/hospital reformer)
Doctors Without Borders (Nobel Peace Prize winner)
Karl Marx, *Das Kapital* (revolution in economics)
Christianity as revolution in religion and culture
Leakey, modern anthropology and archaeology, human
beginning in Africa
Independence movements of 1990s, Bosnia, Yugoslavia

Please use this list for ideas. You are not limited to these topics. Always check with your teacher.

Topics
"Rights and Responsibilities in History"
(NHD theme for 2003)

I. American History

Abigail and John Adams
First Amendment rights, many topics
Water rights in the American West
John Muir, saving the environment
Mormons, freedom of religion in America
T. Roosevelt and "trust busting"
Margaret Sanger, birth control, also child labor
FHA, HUD, federal responsibility for housing
Horace Mann, state responsibility for public education
Women's suffrage, 19th Amendment
Medal of Honor winners
Thurgood Marshall, Brown vs. Board of Education
Cesar Chavez, rights of migrant workers
Andrew Carnegie, Carnegie libraries
Herbert Hoover, Federal Bureau of Investigation
Peace Corps, American responsibility to the world
Civil Rights Movement, freedom riders, lunch counters
Kennedy family, responsibility to serve
Immigrants, tenements, and slum lords
Women in sports, Title IX
New Deal agencies: WPA, Social Security, etc.
Thomas Paine, pamphleteer
Income Tax, paying for government
Little Rock Central High, integration crisis
American Civil Liberties Union, defending civil rights
Andrew Jackson and Indian Removal, the Trail of Tears
Labor unions, strikes, and strike-breakers, many topics
Scopes Trial, right to teach evolution in Tennessee
Puritans in New England, Anne Hutchinson
National Organization of Women and the Equal Rights Amendment, 1970s
J. Robert Oppenheimer, Manhattan Project leader, and responsibility of scientists in atomic weapons research
Bilingual education in America
Nat Tuner, slave rebellion
Abolitionists and anti-slavery movement, 1800–1860
John Peter Zenger, freedom of the press
Draft riots, conscientious objectors, draft dodgers—Civil War, WWII, Vietnam
Ben Franklin, freedom, rights, and civic responsibility
Jane Addams, Hull House, rights of immigrants
Ida B. Wells, journalist, crusade against lynching
Tennessee Valley Authority, public utilities
Rural Electrification, 1930s
McCarthyism and free speech during the Cold War

II. World History

French Revolution and the Rights of Man
Henry II of England and Thomas à Becket
NATO and the Cold War
India, British colony, independence movement, Gandhi
Parnell and Irish independence movement
Greenpeace
John Locke, philosopher, "right to rebel", 18th century
Feudal System, medieval rights and responsibilities
British East India Company, rights and profits
Geneva Convention, rights of POWs
"White Man's Burden", responsibilities of colonialism
Society for the Prevention of Cruelty to Animals
Noblesse oblige, responsibilities of wealth and rank
Slave trade in Britain, John Newton ("Amazing Grace")
Bartólome de las Casas, Indian rights in Mexico, 1500s
Amnesty International
Doctors Without Borders, Nobel Peace Prize winner
Adam Smith and the right to free trade
Caste system in India
Magna Carta, 1215
English Bill of Rights, 1689
Karl Marx, rights and responsibilities of workers
China, restricting reproductive rights
Spanish Inquisition, orthodoxy vs. dissent
Quebec, rights of minority in Canada
Emmeline Pankhurst, women's suffrage in England
Nazi Germany, rights for some, none for others
Greek city states, rights and responsibilities of citizens
Andrei Sakharov, human rights in the USSR
Mexican Revolution, 1910–1920, rights of campesinos
United Nations, Universal Declaration of Human Rights
League of Nations, right of self-determination
Nuremberg trials, Nazi war criminals
International Red Cross
Partition of Palestine, modern Israel
Eastern Europe in Cold War, Iron Curtain, many topics
Fidel Castro and communism in Cuba
Protestant Reformation, Martin Luther, Germany, 1517
John Calvin, John Knox, religion and government
Enclosure movement in England, loss of common land
Charles Dickens, social reform through literature
Australia, prison colony to independent country
Generals' Plot to kill Adolf Hitler, WWII
Declaration of Chapultepec, 1945
Pan American Union, Organization of American States

Please use this list for ideas. You are not limited to these topics. Always check with your teacher.

NHD
NATIONAL
HISTORY DAY

ENTRY # _____

JUDGE _____

TIME _____

ROOM _____

TITLE _____

JUDGING CRITERIA (Judging criteria are explained in the *Student Contest Guide*)	EVALUATION		
	SUPERIOR	EXCELLENT	GOOD
Historical Quality (60%)			
• Entry is historically accurate			
• Shows analysis and interpretation			
• Places topic in historical context			
• Shows wide research			
• Uses **available** primary sources			
• Research is balanced			
Relation to Theme (20%)			
• Clearly relates topic to theme			
• Demonstrates **significance of topic in history** and draws conclusions			
Clarity of Presentation (20%)			
• Exhibit, written material is original, clear, appropriate, organized			
• Exhibit is organized, has visual impact, correctly uses maps, photos, etc.			

Rules Compliance	Yes	No
• Maintains size requirement (40"x30"x72")		
• Includes annotated bibliography		
• Media device maintains time limit (3 mins.)		
• Maintains word limit (500 words)		
• Other:		

Overall Rating (circle one)

Superior   Excellent   Good

COMMENTS
• STRENGTHS
• AREAS FOR IMPROVEMENT

NHD
NATIONAL
HISTORY DAY

ENTRY # _____

JUDGE _____

TIME _____

ROOM _____

TITLE _____

JUDGING CRITERIA (Judging criteria are explained in the *Student Contest Guide*)	EVALUATION		
	SUPERIOR	EXCELLENT	GOOD
Historical Quality (60%)			
• Entry is historically accurate			
• Shows analysis and interpretation			
• Places topic in historical context			
• Shows wide research			
• Uses **available** primary sources			
• Research is balanced			
Relation to Theme (20%)			
• Clearly relates topic to theme			
• Demonstrates **significance of topic in history** and draws conclusions			
Clarity of Presentation (20%)			
• Paper, written material is original, clear, appropriate, organized, well-presented			
• Text is clear, grammatical, and spelled correctly; entry is neatly prepared			

Rules Compliance	Yes	No
• Maintains length requirement (1500-2500 words)		
• Includes annotated bibliography		
• Other:		

Overall Rating (circle one)

Superior   Excellent   Good

COMMENTS
• STRENGTHS
• AREAS FOR IMPROVEMENT

NHD
NATIONAL
HISTORY DAY

ENTRY # _____

JUDGE _____

TIME _____

ROOM _____

TITLE _____

PERFORMANCE

COMMENTS

- STRENGTHS
- AREAS FOR IMPROVEMENT

JUDGING CRITERIA (Judging criteria are explained in the *Student Contest Guide*)	SUPERIOR	EXCELLENT	GOOD
Historical Quality (60%)			
• Entry is historically accurate			
• Shows analysis and interpretation			
• Places topic in historical context			
• Shows wide research			
• Uses **available** primary sources			
• Research is balanced			
Relation to Theme (20%)			
• Clearly relates topic to theme			
• Demonstrates **significance of topic in history** and draws conclusions			
Clarity of Presentation (20%)			
• Presentation, written material is original, clear, appropriate, organized, articulate			
• Performers show good stage presence; props, costumes are historically accurate			

Rules Compliance	Yes	No
• Maintains time requirement (10 mins.)		
• Includes annotated bibliography		
• All equipment, effects are student-run		
• Other:		

Overall Rating (circle one)

Superior   **Excellent**   **Good**

NHD
NATIONAL
HISTORY DAY

ENTRY # _____

JUDGE _____

TIME _____

ROOM _____

TITLE _____

COMMENTS
- STRENGTHS
- AREAS FOR IMPROVEMENT

JUDGING CRITERIA (Judging criteria are explained in the *Student Contest Guide*)	EVALUATION		
	SUPERIOR	EXCELLENT	GOOD
Historical Quality (60%)			
• Entry is historically accurate			
• Shows analysis and interpretation			
• Places topic in historical context			
• Shows wide research			
• Uses **available** primary sources			
• Research is balanced			
Relation to Theme (20%)			
• Clearly relates topic to theme			
• Demonstrates **significance of topic in history** and draws conclusions			
Clarity of Presentation (20%)			
• Presentation, written material is original, clear, appropriate, organized, articulate			
• Entry is organized, visual impact/ documentary category is appropriate to topic			

Rules Compliance	Yes	No
• Maintains time requirement (10 mins.)		
• Includes annotated bibliography		
• All equipment student-run		
• Other:		

Overall Rating (circle one)

Superior   **Excellent**   **Good**

Glossary of History Fair Terms

Advanced competition—any contest beyond the school campus. In most cases first and second place winners, plus certain special awards, advance to the next level.

Annotated Bibliography—required for all History Fair projects. Uses standard bibliographic form, but adds a brief description of how each source was used in the development of the project. Primary sources are separated out and listed first, then secondary sources, both in alphabetic order.

Annotation—the one to three sentence description of a source in the Annotated Bibliography. Annotations for primary sources should also explain why the source is primary to the topic.

Balanced research—has two meanings in History Fair: The student should research and present both sides of a story or an issue. Also, the types of sources used should be varied. For example, a student would not want to depend only on Internet sources, but would "balance" the research by using a number of books and/or magazine articles.

Bibliography—a list of sources used in the development of the project whether for information or for illustration. Entries should be cited in standard form following either Turabian or the Modern Language Association style guides.

Category—the type of presentation the student chooses. National History Day recognizes seven categories: Papers, Individual Exhibit, Group Exhibit, Individual Performance, Group Performance, Individual Documentary, and Group Documentary. Each is a separate competition.

Call-backs—finals. When a project makes the final round of competition, the student(s) is "called back" to present the project and/or be interviewed again for a fresh team of judges to determine the winners.

Cite/Citation—listing the information required when a source is entered in the bibliography or giving credit to the source within a paper. In the required Annotated Bibliography each source has both a citation and an annotation.

Coach—the teacher or sponsor for a student project. Also, to guide and assist a student preparing for competition.

Contest Guide—now called the *Rule Book*. Contains the official National History Day rules.

Curriculum Book—a magazine published annually by National History Day to assist teachers in explaining the NHD theme. It usually contains an essay about the theme, plus articles and lessons using example topics and explaining research techniques.. (Note: This publication was formerly called the "Annual Supplement".)

Division—in History Fair competition contestants are separated into two divisions depending on their school grade level. "Junior Division" is grades six through eight and "Senior Division" is grades nine through twelve.

Document—usually refers to a primary source in print form such as a letter, a bill, or an advertisement.

Documentary—the National History Day category which includes all audiovisual presentation formats, including video tape, slide show, and computer program. In the Documentary category students must run all electronic equipment; no live narration is allowed; and the project must not be interactive as the judges cannot assist in any way. Students may enter the Documentary category as individuals or in groups of two to five. (Note: the Documentary category was formerly called "Media.")

Executive Director—the person responsible for administering the National History Day competition. Dr. Cathy Gorn at the University of Maryland, College Park, has served as Executive Director since 1992.

Exhibit—the National History Day category which combines illustrations, graphics and text to tell the story. Exhibits should resemble museum displays and are limited only in size and the number of student written words. Students may enter the Exhibit category either as individuals or in groups of two to five. (Note: This category was formerly called simply "Projects.")

Finals/Finalists—in competition, the top group of projects in any category from which the winners are chosen. Finals usually indicates a second round of competition with a fresh team of judges.

Group (categories)—students may enter competition as groups of two to five in the Exhibit, Performance, or Documentary categories. The group prepares one project, one Process Narrative, and one Annotated Bibliography of their combined efforts.

History Fair—the all inclusive term to designate National History Day style competition at the campus or district level and the instructional program to prepare and guide students in research and development of their projects.

Historical context—the setting in which project events take place. Includes the social, political, and cultural climate. It also refers to the interaction between the topic and other historical events of the time.

Historical Papers—the National History Day category in which students present their story in traditional written format. Creative writing such as fictional diaries or poems are also acceptable if they adhere to historical fact and conform to all other NHD rules.

Historical perspective—includes how a topic changes over time and what its impact was on other events or people.

Individual (categories)—students prepare their projects and compete alone. There are four individual categories: Exhibits, Papers, Performances, and Documentaries.

Interview—students who enter the Performance or Documentary categories will be asked questions by the judges based on their presentation and paperwork. This "interview" usually lasts five to ten minutes. At advanced levels of competition all contestants may be interviewed by the judges.

Junior Division—according to National History Day rules, contestants are separated into two "divisions" based on their grade level in school. Junior Division includes students in grades six through eight.

Level—as in "advanced levels" of competition, refers to campus, school district, regional, state or national contests.

National History Day—the nationwide program administered through the NHD offices at the University of Maryland, College Park. The annual national competition lasts four days and is usually held the second week of June on the UM campus in College Park near Washington, DC.

Oral history—includes personal memories, stories, recollections, or eyewitness accounts of events and ways of life during the lifetime of the person being interviewed. Usually documented by recording, then transcribing the interview.

Paper—as category, see Historical Papers. Also used to refer to the required process paper.

Performance—the National History Day category in which students prepare original, live, dramatic presentations to tell their story. Both individuals and groups may enter the Performance category. Time limit is ten minutes.

Place—rank in finals as determined by the judges. Also refers to first or second prize which qualifies projects to advance to the next level of competition.

Plagiarism—using the words or ideas of others without giving proper credit. Any student who commits plagiarism is subject to disqualification at all levels of competition.

Primary source—any firsthand information from participants, witnesses, or other sources contemporary to the event being researched.

Process Narrative—term used in this workbook for the one to two page "process paper" required by the National History Day rules for all categories except Papers.

Process paper—a one to two page description of how the topic fits the theme and how the project was researched and developed. The limit is 500 words. Process papers are required for Exhibits, Performances, and Documentaries.

Project—any entry in a History Fair or National History Day competition. (Note: "Project" was formerly used to designate the Exhibit category.)

Project number—usually assigned at the time of registration and determines the location and/or time a project is exhibited or presented. This number should be placed on the title page of project paperwork.

Qualify—refers to the first or second prize in a category as these places "qualify" the project to advance to the next level of competition.

Quote—the exact words from a person, document or a work of literature. Quotes should always be credited with the source and date (if possible). On Exhibits, words in quotes do not count in the 500 word limit because they are not student composed.

Rule Book—the National History Day publication which contains the official rules of competition. These are followed at all levels of advanced competition. Copies can be ordered from the NHD executive office - see Resources. (Note: This publication was formerly titled "NHD Contest Guide.")

Secondary source—information written, or otherwise created, in a time after the event(s) being researched by people who were neither participants nor witnesses.

Senior Division—according to National History Day rules, contestants are separated into two "divisions" based on their grade level in school. Senior Division includes students in grades nine through twelve.

Size limit—applies only to Exhibits which can be no larger than 40 inches wide, 30 inches deep, and 72 inches tall, when displayed.

Special Award—prizes awarded to projects based on specific research or topic criteria. Examples include the Oral History Award and the Colonial Dames Award for projects dealing with colonial and revolutionary American history. Most Special Awards are open to all categories.

Sponsor—the teacher who instructs the students, oversees the development of their projects, and chaperones them at advanced competition. Also called "coach."

State Coordinator—the state equivalent of the National Executive Director; administers the State History Day competition and supervises the History Fair program within the state.

Style Manual/Style Guide—an instruction book

explaining how to prepare written manuscripts, cite various types of sources, and write bibliographies. The most widely accepted are Kate L. Turabian and the Modern Language Association or MLA.

Theme—at the beginning of each contest year the National History Day directors announce a broad, general concept to which all entries must adhere. Some examples are "Frontiers in History," "Triumph and Tragedy in History," and "Science, Technology and Invention in History."

Time limit—applies to Performance and Documentary categories. Both carry a ten minute limit for the presentation, plus five minutes to set up and five minutes to take down equipment or props.

Title page—required for all projects. Information for the title page includes the student name(s) - except at a campus History Fair where judges may be faculty members - the project title, category, and project number. The title page should be plain white paper; no border, color, or decoration of any kind is allowed.

Word limit—on Exhibits and in Process Narratives the limit is 500 words. In an Historical Paper the limit is 2500 words, with a minimum of 1500 words.

Bibliography

Berry, Margaret, and Patricia S. Morris. *Stepping into Research! A Complete Research Skills Activities Program for Grades 5-12.* West Nyack, NY: The Center for Applied Research in Education, 1990.

Black, Mary S. "Internet Research Projects Increase Student Learning without Teacher Hassle" *The Social Studies Texan.* Fall/Winter 1996, pp. 40-41. (Texas Council for the Social Studies).

Corley, Julie A. "Can the Web Really Do It All? Perceptions of Historical Research on the Internet" *Public Historian*, Number 20, Winter 1998, pp. 49-57.

Engines of Inquiry: A Practical Guide for Using Technology to Teach American Culture. American Studies Crossroads Project, Georgetown University, Washington, DC.

Gorn, Cathy. "Getting Caught Up in the Web: Computer Technology, the Internet and National History Day" *Science, Technology, Invention in History: Impact, Influence, Change.* 1999 National History Day Curriculum Book, pp. 16-19.

Hardy, Bea. "National History Day 2001" *Magazine of History.* (Organization of American Historians) Vol. 15, No. 1, Fall 2000, pp. 57-58.

Harris, Robert. "Evaluating Internet Research Sources" (the CARS Checklist) *Science, Technology, Invention in History: Impact, Influence, Change.* 1999 National History Day Curriculum Book, pp. 20-23.

"The Internet and You," *Art to Zoo.* March/April 1997. Published by the Smithsonian Office of Education, Washington, DC.

Kohl, Martha. "A Step-by-Step Guide to Writing a Good History Day Paper" *Magazine of History.* (Organization of American Historians) Vol. 6, No. 4, Spring 1992, pp. 83-86.

Lake, Matt. "Desperately Seeking Something" *Houston Chronicle*, September 18, 1998, p. 1 & 4 G. (reprinted from the *New York Times*)

Marius, Richard. *A Short Guide to Writing about History.* Glenview, IL: Scott, Foresman and Company, 1989.

National Council for the Social Studies. *Expectations of Excellence: Standards for the Social Studies.* Washington, DC: NCSS, 1994.

National Council for the Social Studies. "NCSS Position Statement on Assessment of Social Studies Students." (draft paper) September, 2000.

National History Day. "Using Oral History for National History Day Projects." *Turning Points in History: People, Ideas, Events.* National History Day Curriculum Book 2000. College Park, MD: National History Day, 1999, pp. 20-28.

National History Day. "What Is National History Day" *Migration in History*. National History Day Curriculum Book 1998. College Park, MD: National History Day, 1997, pp. 4-5.

Perkins, Donald. "The Study of History and Cyberspace: The Case of the Armadillo World Web Server" *Insight*. (Newsletter of the Educational Services, Texas State Historical Association) Vol. 10, Spring 1997, pp. 2-5.

Ragsdale, Ken. "Student's Guide to Historical Research and Writing" *Insight*. (Newsletter of the Educational Services, Texas State Historical Association) Vol. 7, Spring 1994, pp. 6-10.

Risinger, C. Frederick. "Separating Wheat from Chaff: Why Dirty Pictures Are Not the Real Dilemma in Using the Internet to Teach Social Studies" *Social Education* (National Council for the Social Studies) Vol. 62, No. 3, March 1998, pp. 148-150.

Simpson, Michael, and Steven S. Lapham. "NHD: National History Day" *Social Education*. (National Council for the Social Studies) Vol. 65, No. 5, September 2001, pp. 320-324.

Texas Historical Commission. "Fundamentals of Oral History: Texas Preservation Guidelines." Austin: Texas Historical Commission, 1999.

Weitzman, David. *My Backyard History Book*. Boston: Little, Brown, 1975.

Index

About the Author

Carlita Kosty organized her first History Fair in 1987 and has been working with the program ever since. She teaches the History Fair program in her classes, presents teacher training workshops, serves as a state History Fair judge, and coaches students for advanced competition. Her students were National History Day finalists in 1999 and 2001.

A graduate of Southwestern University in Georgetown, Texas, Kosty has taught social studies in Texas public schools since 1964. She has served as history department chair in high school and middle school and has written curriculum for a variety of special projects. She lives with her husband Don in San Antonio where she teaches eighth grade American history and runs the school History Fair.